D1072659

The films of
MEL BROOKS

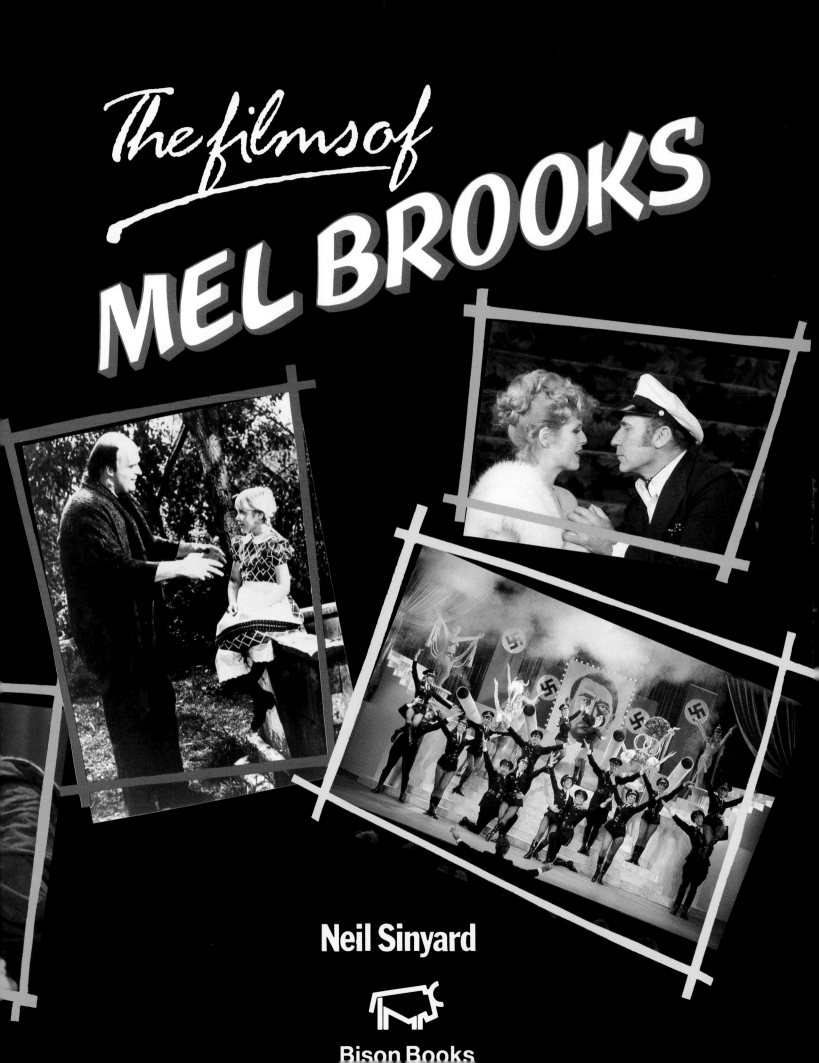

The films of MEL BROOKS

Neil Sinyard

Bison Books

Published by
Bison Books Ltd
176 Old Brompton Road
London SW5 0BA
England

Copyright © 1987 Bison Books Ltd

All rights reserved. No part of this publication may be
reproduced, stored in a retrieval system or transmitted,
in any form, by any means, electronic, mechanical,
photocopying or otherwise, without the written
permission of the publisher.

ISBN 0-86124-384-6

Printed in Hong Kong

CONTENTS

INTRODUCTION

Mel Brooks is a one-man riot. Laughter does not ripple in Brooks: it explodes. The man himself is a shameless show-off, an exuberant exhibitionist who does not simply hug the spotlight but well nigh strangles it.

Brooks arouses strong feelings among critics, some of whom find his scatological sallies puerile and even offensive. In their eyes it is not simply a case of 'anything goes,' it is a case of everything went – taste, discipline, decorum, etc. Brooks has often been accused of bad taste, even by his own characters. ('Well, talk about bad taste!' says an elderly lady as she leaves the auditorium after witnessing the 'Springtime for Hitler' routine in *The Producers*.) He has a stock indignant reply to such shameful accusations – 'Up yours!'

In fact, it is a purpose of this book to show that Brooks's humor stems not from a desire to outrage as much as from a deeply felt rage within himself. He often jokes about the inadequacy of the body as an instrument to reflect the potential of the spirit, but when he ridicules Nazism in *The Producers*, greed in *The Twelve Chairs*, racism in *Blazing Saddles* and persecution in *History of the World – Part I*, there is a seriousness beneath the surface and the farce should not be confused with frivolity. The so-called tastelessness is designed to disturb and to provoke. In any case it was Picasso who said, 'Good taste is the enemy of all art.'

For all the critical controversy over his films, Brooks has been the most influential and successful of American comedy film-makers over the past two decades – alongside Woody Allen, that is. Comparisons between Brooks and Allen are always being made and they seem unavoidable, largely since the development of their careers has been so similar. Both were writers on Sid Caesar's TV comedy special *Your Show of Shows* and both branched out into successful night-club acts. After tentative beginnings in the film industry (Allen as writer and actor, Brooks as inspired commentator on an avant-garde cartoon), both quickly became directors in order to protect their own scripts and also developed as performers in their own films. In their movies one can sometimes detect a similarity of interest – each has his genre parody (*Sleeper, Blazing Saddles*), his send-up of Russian literature (*Love and Death, The Twelve Chairs*), his exercise in styles from the past (*Zelig, Silent Movie*). One can even detect a similarity of problems, notably with film narrative. Can Woody integrate the need for a plot with his one-liners and personal philosophizing? Can Mel tell a story while accommodating his relish for seeming ad-lib spontaneity and the big production number?

Yet the differences are equally significant. Mel has put it this way: 'Woody is poetic, but he's also a critic. I'm not a critic. I can't just zing a few arrows at life as it thunders by. I have to be down on the ground, shouting at it, grabbing it by the horns, biting it.' To parallel their musical prowess with the character of their films, Woody Allen's movies are soulful clarinet solos while Mel Brooks bangs his own drum (skillfully, one might add, although he chose it 'because it was the loudest instrument in the band'). Woody provokes affection and admiration for his cleverness and humanity, but Mel can have you falling off your chair. If Woody is a whiner, Mel is a howler. If Woody's Jewish humor tends toward introspection

or self-deprecation, Mel's Jewish humor rolls over you with raucous aggression. Woody says, 'Pity me, please'; Mel says, 'Pay attention, why don't you?' Woody's comedy is framed around melancholy romance between the sexes, while Mel's is often framed around a close relationship between two men. Woody's humor has evolved toward a reflection of adult complexity, whereas Mel's has seemed more of a conscious regression, in an endeavor to regain the instinctive and innocent wisdom of the child.

'We were so poor, my mother couldn't afford to have me,' said Mel, 'the lady next door gave birth to me.' He was born Melvin

ABOVE: Mel Brooks in a characteristically extrovert pose.

7

ABOVE: Mel Brooks in expansive mood at a press conference.

Kaminsky on 28 June 1926 in New York, the youngest of four sons. Mel's parents were first generation Russian immigrants. Two factors about his childhood might well have had some influence on his later work. The first was the death of his father when Mel was only two. 'I can't tell you what sadness, what pain it is, never to have known my own father,' Mel has said. 'Maybe in having the male characters in my movies find each other, I'm expressing the longing I feel to find my father and be close to him.' Despite this blow, he seems nevertheless to have had a very happy childhood, so much so that he has ascribed his later breakdown and six-year spell under psychoanalysis as having been caused by his grief about the need to grow up and adjust to adulthood. Something of this struggle is dramatized most ingeniously in his spoof psychoanalytical thriller *High Anxiety* and it makes it one of his most sensitive and interesting works.

During his childhood and adolescence Mel's quick wit and freakish sense of humor seemed to suggest he was cut out for show business and, after a brief period of service in World War II, he became a drummer for a dance band and then the replacement for the resident comic. In the process he changed his name to the snappier sounding Melvin Brooks ('Kaminsky' did not fit easily into his opening number where he would introduce himself to his audience, and 'Brooks' was a shortened version of his mother's maiden name Brookman). It was at this time that he became friends with Sid

Caesar who, when signed up for his extraordinarily successful series *Your Show of Shows*, eventually managed to ensure that Mel was recruited as a full-time writer. He joined a team that included Woody Allen, Neil Simon and Larry Gelbart, so competition for the star's approval was fierce.

The experience of the show was an extraordinary training ground for Mel but, as he put it, he found he was getting 'high anxiety' – ascending his profession too fast. He was successful enough to be earning $5000 a week, but he was also turning into an anxious wreck. After *Your Show of Shows* closed his career began grinding to a temporary halt, he was under analysis and his marriage to a young dancer, Florence Baum, which had produced three children, was breaking down. A musical which he had substantially rewritten, *Shinbone Alley* (1957), failed on Broadway; a film script by Brooks commissioned by Jerry Lewis for his film *The Ladies Man* (released in 1961) was entirely thrown out. By the end of the 1950s Brooks's average weekly salary had slumped to an unemployment check of $85. If he had believed Scott Fitzgerald's famous aphorism that 'there are no second acts in American lives' he would have been in deep trouble. In fact, Brooks's career has had at least three acts.

He was rescued on this occasion by a 2000-Year-Old Man, one of a number of routines he had developed with his friend Carl Reiner for entertaining at parties. An old man who was present at the Crucifixion would talk about life and about the people he knew – Christ ('He came in the store, He never bought anything, He always had twelve guys with Him'), Robin Hood ('he stole from everybody and kept everything'), Joan of Arc ('I went with her'), Shakespeare ('What a pussycat!') For Reiner the fun was in the spontaneity and the reactions Brooks would come up with when Reiner lobbed him unexpected questions – 'a brilliant mind going into panic,' was the way Reiner described it. The fame of the routine grew. The distinguished theater critic Kenneth Tynan stumbled into a performance and immediately labelled Brooks as 'the most original comic improviser I have ever seen.' George Burns told Brooks about his routine that 'you'd better record it or I'm going to steal it.' The 2000-Year-Old Man was duly to appear on three hugely popular records and an animated cartoon version of some of the sketches was also made. All this led Brooks to a series of improvised beer commercials with the talk-show host Dick Cavett, which also became instant classics.

The upturn in Brooks's career was matched in his private life. In 1964 he married the actress Anne Bancroft whom he had met in 1961 while attending a recording of her appearance in *The Perry Como Show*. 'I know you're wondering how I got her,' says Brooks cheekily to interviewers when they ask about his marriage, as if he is a little sensitive about the question. On the face of it, it seems one of the unlikeliest showbiz marriages since Arthur Miller and Marilyn Monroe, yet by all accounts it has been a very happy one. Also (let us hope he is reading this) Brooks has been growing handsomer over the years. His appearances in *The Twelve Chairs* and *Blazing Saddles* are fairly grotesque, but by the time of *High Anxiety* he is beginning to blossom into a likeable, romantic hero.

Brooks's first cinematic success came when he improvised a commentary on a brilliant cartoon by Ernest Pintoff called *The Critic* (1963). A series of avant-garde, abstract, Norman McClaren-like shapes appear on the screen; a seventy-year-old cinemagoer, audibly and to the annoyance of others in the audience, tries to make sense of what he is seeing. Is this shape a cockroach? Is it a dirty picture? 'I think this is some kind of symbolism,' says the voice as yet another odd image emerges. The image crystallizes into a drawing of a table. 'I think it's supposed to be symbolizing junk.' Far from symbolizing junk *The Critic* went on to win the Oscar for the best animated short of 1963. Mel Brooks's career in films had begun.

ABOVE: Mel Brooks: ever the comedian.

LEFT: Mel Brooks arrives at a premiere.

THE PRODUCERS

1967

RIGHT: Leo (Gene Wilder, left) and Max (Zero Mostel, right) try to bring a distraught Franz Liebkind (Kenneth Mars, center) under control in *The Producers*.

BELOW: Leo and Max gratefully remove their Nazi armbands after their first meeting with the author of the worst play ever written. From *The Producers*.

Asked if it was hard to convince people that he should be allowed to direct *The Producers*, Mel Brooks replied, 'About as hard as it is for a Jew to check into the Cairo Hilton.' Like a lot of eminent Hollywood writer-directors, such as Preston Sturges, Billy Wilder and Joseph L Mankiewicz, Brooks's primary motive for going into direction was simply that he thought it the best way to protect his own script. Fortunately he was enthusiastically supported by an independent producer, Sidney Glazier, to whom he had been introduced by a mutual friend, Barry Levinson. Levinson, incidentally, himself a highly skilled film and

television writer, was to play the bellboy who attacks Brooks in the shower in *High Anxiety* and was also to move into film direction with works like *Diner* (1982) and *The Natural* (1984). Glazier raised some of the money and the rest was put up by movie tycoon Joseph Levine, who was at that time riding high on the enormous success of *The Graduate* (1967).

At this stage the title was *Springtime for Hitler* but it was changed during production to *The Producers*, probably because the original title might not only have conveyed the wrong impression but, more importantly, given away in advance the film's best joke. Brooks originally intended to play the part of the German playwright, Franz Liebkind, himself, but Kenneth Mars's reading of the part at the audition was so good that the role went to him. The other main casting problem was Zero Mostel in the leading role because, by all accounts, he and Brooks had clashes of ego and found it hard to get along. 'Shut up, I'm having a rhetorical conversation!' says Mostel's character at one stage. The comment more or less encapsulates the relationship between star and director, a relationship which is to leave an impact on the film itself.

The plot is, by now, well known. With the aid of his nervous new accountant Leo Bloom (Gene Wilder), the theatrical producer Max Bialystock (Zero Mostel) is brought to realize that there is probably more money to be made from a flop than a success. The reason is that there are no profits to be paid to your enthusiastic backers to whom you have offered a percentage, and therefore you can pocket their stake yourself. The search is on for the

world's worst play. 'Remember,' Max tells Leo as he feverishly flicks through a multitude of texts, 'this play has got to close by page four.'

Kafka's *Metamorphosis* is rejected, even though Max does not get beyond the first sentence ('Gregor Samsa awoke one morning to find himself transformed into a giant cockroach . . .'). But their prayers seem to have been answered by their discovery of *Springtime for Hitler*, a tribute to the Führer written by a mad Nazi who lives reclusively in a seedy New York apartment. To make their flop fail-safe they then recruit the most unsuitable director, Roger De Bris (Christopher Hewett), a specialist in musical comedy who perhaps has a limited grasp of the work's historical basis: 'That whole third act has got to go . . . they're losing the war, it's so depressing.' When a hippy vocalist, Lorenzo St Dubois, or LSD (Dick Shawn) is cast as a wildly improbable Hitler, everything seems in place for a disaster of mammoth proportions. But there's no business like show business and no accounting for public taste and things do not exactly go according to plan.

Much of the humor of the film stems initially from the broadness of the stereotypes.

ABOVE: Max succumbs to the charms of a merry widow (Estelle Winwood) in *The Producers*.

RIGHT: Success is the best revenge? Max and Leo muse over their fate in *The Producers*.

Indeed, for all the egomania of Max and the neurosis of Leo, the two heroes become symbols of near-normality the more they penetrate the bizarre world of the theater. Each of the main theatrical madmen – playwright, producer and performer – is given his own little comic cadenza to demonstrate a mind that is coming off its hinges and each actor responds to his opportunity superbly. With his war helmet and warbled oscillations between 'Deutschland über alles,' and 'Yankee Doodle Dandy,' Kenneth Mars's Franz is nutty Nazism personified, raging against Churchill and insisting that Hitler, at the very least, was a better painter ('He could paint an entire apartment in one afternoon – two coats!') Christopher Hewett's creative genius, Roger, first appears before Max and Leo in a dress, and epitomizes theater at its most effete, self-absorbed and socially remote: 'I never knew the Third Reich meant Germany ... it's drenched with historical goodies like that.' As LSD, Dick Shawn excels in a soulful rendering of the parody protest song 'The Power of Love,' which details the horrid fate of LSD's flower of peace and contains such life-enhancing utterances as, 'Hey world, you stink/Man, it's later than you think.' These set-pieces are augmented by a memorably eccentric audition scene in which a multitude of

miniature, aspiring Hitlers ('no previous experience required,' says the casting call) attempt to catch the casting director's eye with songs that range from 'Beautiful Dreamer' to 'A Wandering Minstrel, I.'

There are two basic targets of the humor here. The first is the whole period of the late 1960s, with its attitudes of protest, its atmosphere of tastelessness and its adulation of camp. In fact, the ultimate, ironic success of Max and Leo's show is not that implausible. In the age of *The Rocky Horror Picture Show* it is clear that the appeal of the appalling has always been quite powerful. It is also a comment on middle-class audiences of the time

ABOVE: Bialystock and Bloom acquire a secretary (Lee Meredith) in *The Producers*.

who desperately wanted to appear 'with-it' and who were often quite prepared to applaud the phony if it appeared also to be fashionable.

Brooks's other immediate target is the pretentiousness of the 1960s' musical. *Springtime for Hitler* particularly mocks *The Sound of Music* (1965) which also sets jolly songs against a fascist backdrop. More generally, the film calls into question some of the utopian assumptions of the musical which traditionally is a form that celebrates hope, success, freedom and love. By way of contrast and counterpoint, *The Producers* is a musical comedy about fear and failure, with no love story and recurrent imagery of prison. It is not about sweet charity – it is about desperate fraud.

The main thrust of the comedy, however, is undoubtedly its attack on Nazism, an obsession with Brooks which he works into just about everything he films, however incongruous the context (Nazis even crop up in the Wild West of *Blazing Saddles*, for example). 'If I get up on the soapbox and wax eloquently, it'll be blown away in the wind,' he said about the constant allusions to Nazism in his films, 'but if I do *Springtime for Hitler*, it'll never be forgotten.' For Woody Allen, the existence of Nazism is a constant source of philosophical despair in his films, notably in *Stardust Memories* (1980) and *Hannah and Her Sisters* (1986); and for a neurotic clown like Spike Milligan, the absurd figure of Hitler is the ultimate symbol of the modern world's mad malevolence which comedy alone can make bearable. Brooks would understand and sympathize with both of these attitudes, but his predominant response to the phenomenon of fascism is rage. In *The Producers* he attempts to do to Nazism what Chaplin tried in *The Great Dictator* (1940) and what Lubitsch tried in *To Be Or Not To Be* (1942), that is, he holds Nazism up to ridicule in the hope that the corresponding laughter will ensure that such an obscenity can never again be taken seriously as a political philosophy. Everything in the film, therefore, builds toward the stage production of *Springtime for Hitler*, which is to date perhaps his ultimate exercise in black comedy – arguably the funniest thing he has ever done and also, indubitably, the most serious.

The opening production number of the title song includes a Tyrolean chorus; a Nazi tap-dance routine, with a versified verbal

RIGHT: The 'Springtime for Hitler' routine is brought to a triumphant conclusion – still perhaps Mel Brooks's supreme example of exuberant bad taste.

ABOVE: Putting on a show, Nazi-style. From *The Producers*.

insert ('Don't be stupid, be a smartie/Come and join the Nazi party'); and a fervent rendering of the lyrics which include such 'goodies' as, 'We're marching to a faster pace/Look out – here comes the master race.' The audience sits open-mouthed, as well it might. At this juncture, Max and Leo celebrate their catastrophe by retiring to the bar where they are joined by a self-confessed drunken failure who can share their sentiments – a part played, incidentally, by William Hickey who was to be so good as the godfather in John Huston's *Prizzi's Honor* (1985). However, back at the theater, LSD's exchanges with the stage Eva Braun ('I lieb' ye, I lieb' ye, now lieb me alone!') persuade the audience that it is all a joke in the most delightful bad taste. When Max and Leo return and are greeted by the sound of laughter, their faces mask over in pain and at the end they are in tears. 'Where did I go right?' Max will ask.

Toward the end of the title song routine Brooks inserts an aerial shot of the chorus as it spins round in the shape of a swastika. It is a somewhat incongruous shot in the context of the stage performance since it is a joke that would clearly be lost on a theater audience, but it has two particular functions in relation to the comedy of the scene. Nazi ideology is expounded and ridiculed through the incongruity of a dance routine that is pure Busby Berkeley. The outrageousness and even unpleasantness of the material are therefore punctured and undercut by the absurd cheeriness of the musical comedy context (he will do the same in the Inquisition routine in *History of the World – Part I*). On the one hand the comedy works because of the inappropriateness of the comparison; on the other hand though, the comparison is not as inappropriate as one might think. Commenting on Berkeley's technique of molding a multitude of human bodies into patterns of his own devising, critics have mischievously compared his style to that of Leni Riefenstahl in her notorious propaganda films for the Third Reich, notably

Triumph of the Will (1934). Clearly, similar techniques are being put to completely different uses, but Brooks's rather astute coupling of the martial precision of Nazism with the clockwork choreography of Busby Berkeley is a testimony to his ciné-literacy.

If the humor of the film lies mainly with the supporting characters and the set-pieces, the film's heart lies in the relationship between Max Bialystock and Leo Bloom. At first one notices the extreme contrast between them – Max songful, energetic, uninhibited, and Leo quiet and nervous with a little blue blanket for a comforter and a tendency to become so terrified when cornered that not even a dousing with cold water helps ('I'm wet, I'm wet, I'm still hysterical and I'm wet!') As Mel Brooks has explained in an interview in *American Film*, the relationship is essentially that between Ego and Id, mouse and monster. As the film develops the two come closer together. 'Bialystock taught Bloom the ways of greed and the monstrous ways of capitalism,' says Brooks, 'and Bloom taught Bialystock the ways of love and finally melted the ogre's heart like the fable.' It is the first example of a motif that runs right the way through Brooks's work – the love between two men.

ABOVE: Unlike Max who is quite uninhibited, Leo is very, very nervous. From *The Producers*.

LEFT: Look out – here comes the Master Race. From the 'Springtime for Hitler' routine in *The Producers*.

RIGHT: In the theater bar, Leo and Max are aghast to learn that their flop is going down a treat.

BELOW: Hitler (Dick Shawn) and Eva Braun (Renee Taylor) share an intimate moment in the *Springtime for Hitler* production.

ABOVE: After the ridiculing of his masterpiece, the playwright (Kenneth Mars) comes to take revenge on his producers.

In the court scene, when Max and Leo have been found 'incredibly guilty' by the jury, Leo makes a speech on Max's behalf. 'Whom has Max Bialystock wronged?' he asks. '. . . No one ever called me Leo before. This is a wonderful man, he made me what I am today.' True enough, a prisoner, but inwardly freer than before. In an earlier sequence, when they have spent a day in the park behaving like two children on holiday, Leo cannot account for his strange feeling and it is Max who must suggest to him that it might be happiness. To Leo's comment that 'if we get caught, we go to prison,' Max replies, 'Do you think we're not in prison now?' The final shot of the

sequence (reprised in the final image of the film) is that of a fountain surging forth to mimic Leo's ecstasy as he agrees to go along with Max's plan. Leo chants his name in an absurd yet touching declaration of his individualism – an individualism which his new friend alone has released.

All this suggests that we are meant to find Max Bialystock more lovable than is actually the case. Part of the problem is Zero Mostel's over-strenuous and self-enclosed performance, which might be one of the by-products of the strained relationship between Mostel and Brooks mentioned earlier. In general though, Mostel is a brilliant clown, but he rarely elicits pathos. It is not

ABOVE: Max (right) with one of his geriatric financial backers in *The Producers*. He is proclaiming his love; she is having trouble with her hearing aid.

RIGHT: The curvacious cavortings of Ulla (Lee Meredith) are no longer so appealing to Leo and Max now their plan has backfired.

FAR RIGHT: The odd couple: Max and Leo in *The Producers*.

entirely Mostel's fault however that the performance does not work. The character is introduced in a rather sleazy way, essentially as a gigolo for geriatrics with money, and this seems to be Brooks's miscalculation more than Mostel's. Compare, for example, the care and skill with which Billy Wilder establishes sympathy for his hero (Jack Lemmon) in the black comedy *The Apartment* (1960) *before* disclosing the full squalor of his situation. Mostel's opening scene with his procession of wealthy widows is not nearly so funny as a sequence in the middle of the film when he is courting them again to raise money for *Springtime for Hitler* – a courtship which involves a mad motorcyle ride, having to shout 'I love you!' into a hearing-aid in a crowded park, and having to wait an eternity at a widow's front door as she de-activates her numerous burglar alarms. In an emotional sense though, these scenes come in the wrong order. It would be better if Mostel were funny first and pathetic later – here it is the other way round.

To his credit Mel Brooks has acknowledged that he felt he made some mistakes in the structure of *The Producers*. After the *Springtime for Hitler* sequence, the last fifteen minutes are a considerable

anti-climax – the plot developments after the stage performance ought to have been wrapped up much more speedily. The scenes involving Max and his new blond receptionist, Ulla (Lee Meredith), are presumably there to inject a bit of sex appeal but are desperately unfunny. Technically too Brooks came to realize that he still had a lot to learn. Because of a tendency to bunch the close-ups together, the early scenes between Max and Leo can seem ranting and oppressive. John Morris's score is also a little too busy, too insistent in reminding us that this is a comedy and we should be having a good time; later Morris will attune himself superbly to Brooks's style.

The immediate critical response to the film was mixed. The picture was publicized with a rave review by Peter Sellers who had seen it at a private screening and who described it as the 'ultimate film' and 'the

essence of all great comedy combined in a single motion picture.' In contrast, the most influential American critics were mainly hostile, Andrew Saris describing the direction as 'thoroughly inept and vile,' Pauline Kael calling it 'amateurishly crude' and Arthur Schlesinger Jr referring to it ironically as 'an almost flawless triumph of bad taste, unredeemed by wit or by style.' Brooks was understandably wounded by the reaction, but he had the compensation of winning an Oscar for his original screenplay (Gene Wilder was also nominated for his supporting performance). Nowadays *The Producers* looks a more uneven achievement than the very best of Brooks, but with some inspired moments that have deservedly elevated the film to the status of cult classic. What was undeniable was that a distinctive new voice had arrived in screen comedy, and it was loud and unashamed.

THE TWELVE CHAIRS

1970

'*The Producers* was a joyful experience although I may have moved ahead cinematically with *The Twelve Chairs*,' said Brooks in an interview in the magazine *Action*. He went on, 'I think it's a much finer film, in terms of cinema. The shots are more beautiful and the whole ambience, look and texture are more cinematic.' Suddenly that train of thought was not only stopped but began to reverse along the same track: 'But who cares about all that junk? It's really the spirit of the thing that counts. It's whether or not the performances smash across the screen into your heart or into your laugh box and live with you, remain with you.'

And there's the rub. Who cares about the 'junk' of aestheticism if there is nobody in the audience to see it? The discrepancy between aesthetic and commercial achievement in Mel Brooks is at its most extreme in *The Twelve Chairs*. It is his most visually elaborate and beautiful film and also his biggest box-office flop. He does things in the movie that he has never attempted since to anything like the same degree and with the same intensity – that is, the film simultaneously attempts to tell a story, involve the audience with the characters and point a moral. Just as *High Noon* (1952) is often regarded as a western for people who don't like westerns, *The Twelve Chairs* is sometimes seen as a Mel Brooks movie for people who don't like Mel Brooks movies. Conversely, as Nick Smurthwaite has accurately noted in *Mel Brooks and the Spoof Movie*, 'Many confirmed Brooks fans have never heard of it to this day.' It is not an entirely satisfactory movie, but it is a very interesting one and suggests that Brooks's range as both writer and director is wider than has

sometimes been acknowledged by his critics.

The film was shot in Yugoslavia under conditions which seem to have been rather difficult, to say the least. According to Brooks, Belgrade had the only ten-watt bulb; Tito had the car Saturday nights; and the mosquitoes in Brooks's hotel room were so large that they would sit in the armchairs with their legs crossed. However, it was not the conditions of shooting which explain the failure of the film. On the contrary, it is extremely well photographed by Dorde

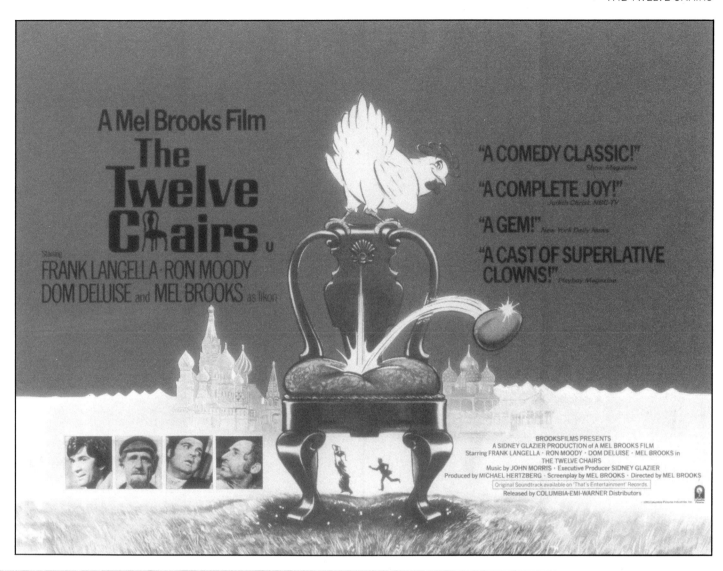

ABOVE: The poster for *The Twelve Chairs*.

LEFT: Mel Brooks in a publicity still for *The Twelve Chairs*.

ABOVE: Having heard the confession of the mother-in-law of Vorobyaninov (Ron Moody, left), Father Fyodor (Dom DeLuise) beats a hasty retreat to search for the jewels. From *The Twelve Chairs*.

Nikolić and the locations contribute greatly to the authentic atmosphere of a story that reads as if the spirit of Billy Wilder had been miraculously let loose in the Soviet society of the immediate post-Revolution period. Wilder's gift as a satirist is the ability to make the jokes emanate from the characters and the situation. It is that gift which is needed here. In Brooks, however, characters and situation have very often to dig themselves out from the weight of the jokes under which they have been buried. In *The Twelve Chairs*, plot, character, humor and morality must complement each other; in Brooks's movies they sometimes get in the way of one another.

The film is based on a classic satirical novel by the Ukrainian writers Ilf (Ilya Faynzilberg) and Petrov (Yevgeny Katayev), which coincidentally was also being adapted for the screen at roughly the same time by the Soviet director, Leonid Gaidai. Brooks had read the novel at the age of fifteen and had been overwhelmed by its wit, reminiscent of Gogol, and its audacity in suggesting – at a time of post-Revolutionary zeal and idealism – that humanity's

innate greed was a more basic instinct than its feelings of fraternity. Set in 1927, ten years after the Revolution, a former nobleman Vorobyaninov (Ron Moody) learns from his dying mother-in-law that she had sewn her precious family jewels into one of the twelve chairs that used to adorn the house in the good old days of the Czar. However, she has also imparted this information to her confessor Father Fyodor (Dom DeLuise) who rapidly finds the temptation of such baubles quite outweighing any religious or moral scruples.

The search will drive Vorobyaninov to a Moscow museum, to a repertory company aboard ship, even to a high-wire act at the circus; Father Fyodor will even brave the wilds of Siberia. During his pursuit Vorobyaninov reluctantly acquires the companionship of a young conman Ostap (Frank Langella) who has discovered the nature of his quest and who threatens to turn him in to the secret police if he does not take him along. The main pursuers will cross paths continuously and the conclusion of their search will be richly ironic.

The film's title song sets the tone, an

BELOW: Tikon laments the abolition of his servitude in *The Twelve Chairs*.

original Mel Brooks composition, with a little bit of melodic help from Brahms, entitled 'Hope for the Best, Expect the Worst.' (Unkind critics have since taken that as a motto for every new Mel Brooks movie.) One memorable verse goes:

> Hope for the best, expect the worst
> You could be Tolstoy – or Fanny Hurst.
> So take your chances
> There are no answers.
> Hope for the best, expect the worst.

The song establishes the witty tone of the film but also, perhaps, its thematic bitterness – a comment on the outcome of the characters' aspirations and maybe even on Brooks's remark on the Russian Revolution itself which set off with such high hopes. Brooks's evocation of post-Revolutionary Russia is a mixture of the surreal, the satirical and the sour. A street sign is seen with the names of Marx, Engels and Lenin celebrated, but with that of Trotsky crossed out. A street cop is glimpsed busily directing the traffic – except there are no cars, only pedestrians. The new society seems to be being half-strangled by a Kafkaesque

bureaucracy turning in upon itself: there is a Bureau of Tables and Chairs, even a Bureau of Bureaus and a huge sign 'Do not waste paper!' in an office that is sinking under its paper weight.

There is a similar combination of humor, sadness and criticism in the characterization and performances. Former nobleman Vorobyaninov, now humble clerk, has a sensitivity that is basically a hot-line to his own egotism. 'That poor woman, that poor woman,' he murmurs when he learns that his mother-in-law is dying, 'who is going to take care of me?' The death-bed scene is a comical but also affecting spectacle of regret and remorse. The old lady murmurs, 'Please forgive me,' and Vorobyaninov, in leaning down to kiss her, inadvertently plants the message 'Cancelled – 17 August 1927' on her cheek with the office stamp attached to his finger. After this his greed will reduce him almost to the level of a wild animal, causing him to growl at people and frequently compelling Ostap to restrain him as if on a leash.

What moderates our disgust at this mercenary bestiality is a brief flashback reverie of his former life. It does not excuse

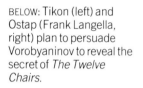

BELOW: Tikon (left) and Ostap (Frank Langella, right) plan to persuade Vorobyaninov to reveal the secret of *The Twelve Chairs*.

his behavior but it does afford an insight into the extent both of his desperation and his degradation. His lowest point comes when he and Ostap are in desperate need of money and the statue of the great Dostoevsky (under which Vorobyaninov poses sadly) gives Ostap the idea that by faking an epileptic fit Vorobyaninov will be able to raise money from sympathetic passersby. The former nobleman is outraged at this suggestion, thinking it beneath his dignity,

and the two come to blows. However, he does it, saying to Ostap afterward, 'When this business is over, I never want to see you again.' Ron Moody's performance is a study in melancholy that occasionally shades into raving depression. Its intensity blocks the release of humor but does penetrate to the character's heart.

Ostap is played by Frank Langella, whose biggest film role to date has been the title character in John Badham's Byronic inter-pretation of *Dracula* (1979). Ostap is suave, narcissistic, a man who thinks quickly both on and off his feet. We first see him minus an eye and a leg, displaying the slogan, 'I left an eye and a leg at the Winter Palace – won't you leave something with me?' However, when a pretty girl passes as charity is being bestowed, an eye is revealed behind his patch, his missing leg is produced from hid-ing and, to his startled benefactor, Ostap says quickly, 'What can I say, little father,

ABOVE: The market in *The Twelve Chairs*. The movie is one of Brooks's most visually elaborate and engaging.

I LEFT AN EYE
AND A LEG AT
THE WINTER PALACE

WON'T YOU LEAVE
SOMETHING WITH ME?

TOP: The one-legged beggar Ostap finds his vision miraculously restored when he spies a pretty girl in *The Twelve Chairs*.

ABOVE: 'I am in lust with you': Ostap romances a young peasant woman (Bridget Price) in *The Twelve Chairs*.

it's a miracle!' before hurrying after the girl. He is similarly adept when the girl's husband returns and their heavy breathing is instantly transformed into a session of artificial respiration, with the emphasis on 'artificial.' At first established as a fleet-footed charlatan, Ostap reveals other sides to his nature as the tale develops. It is clear he is more of an instigator than an actor – it is Vorobyaninov who must perform on stage, walk the tightrope and spin and kick

about in the feigned epileptic fit. Also there is a passion beneath his penury which explodes when Vorobyaninov is mortified by being asked to beg. 'Parasite!' Ostap cries, 'I begged all my life. Pride is a luxury neither of us can afford . . .' One of the main themes of the film is the fluctuating relationship between these two men, at times opportunistic and antagonistic, at other times sympathetic and compassionate. If Vorobyaninov is too selfish and greedy to be the hero, Ostap is too languid and self-regarding, and Langella plays him with a somewhat sickly charm that is highly appropriate. The problem with both performances is that, although they are both intelligently anti-heroic, the effect is that audiences are never really rooting for either of them.

Dom DeLuise's performance as Father Fyodor is on another plane altogether. Nobody has been so completely transformed by the pursuit of gold since Humphrey Bogart in *The Treasure of the Sierra Madre* (1948). He becomes so unhinged that he even unhinges the world around him. During one frantic outburst at the house of a family in Siberia whom he mistakenly believes has the chairs, his behavior is such as to cause a painting to drop off a wall of its own volition. 'A memento of my visit to your beautiful home,' he cries, clinging to a chair as they are trying to drag him on all fours out of their house. (It is another dimension of Brooks's ironic portrayal of the post-Revolutionary society that, for all its professed equality, the characters in the film are so often on their knees or on their backs. 'There will be no grovelling in this house!' Fyodor is told sternly.) His pursuit of the chairs is to deprive him of all values, change his appearance and turn all his prayers into pleas for divine intervention on his behalf. DeLuise plays the part to the hilt and beyond, making moaning noises of orgasmic ecstasy as he senses he is near his treasure.

Brooks comes up with some fine imagery to comment on Father Fyodor's transformation. There is that moment when he arrives in Siberia and opens the train door to be greeted by a literal wall of ice – a joke about the location, of course, but also a quick visual metaphor for the now-frozen state of Fyodor's soul. (Compare Stroheim's symbolic use of the desert for the two characters at the end of his 1923 silent masterpiece *Greed* to suggest how their monetary obsession has dried up the well-springs of their humanity.) There is the character's wonderful coda where he has tracked down what he believes is the elusive chair at the top of a hill. He finds it is not the one he wants ('O Lord – you're so *strict*'), and then discovers he cannot get down. DeLuise delivers the final speech superbly: 'If this is Your punishment . . . How did I get here? There's no way down . . . I'm going to need a great deal of help to get down . . . O, boys! . . . Get me down!' It is a speech that finally acknowledges the human need for companionship ('O, boys!') but his cry after the retreating figures of Ostap and Vorobyaninov dwindles into a hollow echo and he is left stranded in a setting which precisely mirrors his moral state – a self-induced world of alienation and isolation.

Another image that crystallizes his demented wealth obsession is one already mentioned, that of his clinging to the leg of a chair as he is being pulled backward out of a house on his stomach. The significant thing here is that the image is recalled in a different context in the film's final scene, when Vorobyaninov is seen clinging onto a chairback, even though the chair itself is now as shattered as his illusions. For the jewels have already been discovered and used for the benefit of the people – 'a miracle,' as one of them says, a word of which Brooks is fond in his films and which has comic and cruelly ironic overtones in this film. When Vorobyaninov throws away the chair-back he is in effect casting aside that rotten part of his soul that still linked him to Father Fyodor – the clinging greed. His discovery

ABOVE: Vorobyaninov meditates under the statue of the great Dostoevsky in *The Twelve Chairs*.

of humility and his acceptance of his life at the level of the people are also established in this final scene in another image of cruel comedy, the throwing of an epileptic fit, which attracts a curious crowd and persuades Ostap to rejoin his troubled friend and rally support from the spectators – 'Give, give – from the bottom of your heart.'

That final moment, as the camera cranes to reveal Vorobyaninov's contortions on the ground amid the crowd, is Dostoevskian in a number of senses. There is not only the simulation of epilepsy but the kind of situation that recurs many times in Dostoevsky, that is, the desperate action of a despairing character being played out in front of a crowd not simply curious, but killing themselves with laughter. (Think only of such scenes involving Raskolnikov, Marmeladov and his wife in Dostoevky's *Crime and Punishment*.) Dostoevsky might seem a peculiar artist to invoke in a discussion of Mel Brooks, yet both of them have a very acute sense of the thin line that divides tragedy from farce – Dostoevsky sees this from the perspective of a tragedian, Brooks of a farceur – and both of them contain within themselves a bubbling life-force that comes out in their work as chaotic vitality. Coincidentally, the kinds of criticism that have been levelled at Brooks's work – lack of discipline, coarseness, formlessness, shrieking intensity – are almost exactly the same as those levelled at Dostoevsky by critics such as Henry James and Joseph Conrad. And in both cases, their loudness and their melodrama stem from a hatred of death and a burning desire to embrace life.

The final image – Vorobyaninov kicking away but going nowhere, encircled by a fascinated crowd – also completes the motif of mad circles that seems to run through the film. During a struggle over a chair, Father Fyodor and Vorobyaninov pull themselves round in a crazy circle before falling – it is a cameo of their whole action. Similarly, their behavior in ripping the guts out of the chair is, symbolically, a statement of the kind of greed that is ripping apart their own humanity. 'You're not worth spitting on,' says Vorobyaninov to Fyodor, who replies, 'Well, you *are*,' and promptly obliges. The action seems full of exits and returns, of leaving and then having to cover old ground – perpetual motion, but no progress. Even Vorobyaninov's former servant, a lively cameo played by Brooks himself, reinforces this when he falls in a drunken stupor but still moves his legs while flat on the floor, insisting, 'I'm coming, I'm coming.' He has the illusion of movement, but he is going nowhere and is still living in the past anyway and bemoaning the present. ('There isn't a spare bed in the whole of Russia . . . people are sleeping *between* each other . . .') Brooks summarized the theme as 'Governments change, people never . . .' It explains his portrayal of the faltering social dynamic of post-Revolutionary Russia as it finds its socialist idealism trammelled up in the eternal verities of selfishness and avarice. *The Twelve Chairs* not only satirizes self-interest but shows the stark savagery behind it. It might not be his harshest portrait of human nature, but it is his most *overtly* severe. The theme is foregrounded more than the jokes and ultimately overwhelms them; elsewhere in Brooks it is the other way round.

It is interesting to compare *The Twelve*

BELOW: Money before beauty: Father Fyodor prepares to smash a luxurious chair in his search for the jewels in *The Twelve Chairs.*

ABOVE: A frenzied Vorobyaninov (left) and a flimsily disguised Father Fyodor fight over a chair in *The Twelve Chairs*.

Chairs with Woody Allen's affectionate and amusing homage to the Russian classics, *Love and Death* (1975), which is set a century earlier. Both films have a visual elaboration that at that time was unusual for their directors; both have heroes betrayed by fate; and both are fundamentally serious about greed and the vicissitudes of divine justice. Allen's classy cultural allusions are displaced in Brooks's film by frenetic farce and speeded up action that winds up the tension like a coiled spring. Also one can contrast Allen's romanticism (notably in the relationships between characters played by him and Diane Keaton) to Brooks's fraternity, where the main relationships invariably turn out to be male friendships. Although there are moments of tenderness, *The Twelve Chairs* is a curiously loveless film, which is part of its point and poignancy. What the characters want, they cannot have; what they need, they do not want.

BLAZING SADDLES

1974

At one stage in *The Producers* a morose Max Bialystock moans, 'I'm being sunk by a society demanding success when all I can offer is failure.' After the flop of *The Twelve Chairs* Mel Brooks has confessed that he felt rather like that himself and indeed that he thought his career might be through. So *Blazing Saddles* was written out of a sense of fear and anger – what Brooks has described as 'berserk, heartfelt stuff about white corruption and racism and Bible-thumping bigotry . . .'

It succeeded beyond Brooks's wildest dreams. *Blazing Saddles* was the most popular western of the 1970s and also the most destructive; the genre has scarcely recovered since. As in all screen comedy

BELOW: Mel Brooks as Governor William J LePetomane in *Blazing Saddles*. Robyn Hilton plays his secretary, Miss Stein.

some of the success can undoubtedly be attributed to shrewd or fortuitous timing. The film arrived at a time when not only the western was questioning some of its own myths, but when America itself, during the post-Vietnam and post-Watergate period, was also undergoing a session of soul-searching. Brooks's anarchic attitude to heroism and a sense of national destiny therefore seemed to echo a troubled national mood.

On one level *Blazing Saddles* homes in on the modern western's new honesty and anti-romanticism. It might well have taken heart and inspiration from the unprecedented sight of horse dung in Joseph L Mankiewicz's *There was a Crooked Man* (1970). If Sam Peckinpah's *The Wild Bunch* (1969) can be saluted as the western which brought a new realism to the genre's depiction of violence, *Blazing Saddles* can equally be acknowledged as the western with the distinction of bringing a new realism to the genre's attitude to flatulence. 'I mean,' says Brooks, 'you can't eat so many beans without some noise happening there.' He was talking about the famous campfire scene which, in terms of the riotous vulgarity of subsequent screen comedy, was to be an indication of the way the wind was blowing. Warner Brothers wanted to cut the scene entirely, or at least shorten it. Brooks, however, was adamant about leaving it intact, partly because of its authenticity ('we are becoming more and more honest about the activity of the human anatomy,' he explained disarmingly) and partly because the length was essential to the comedy timing. As he explained in his 1975 *Playboy* interview:

'With the first fart, a slight shudder goes through the crowd and you can hear a gasp from the people who are just a little more sensitive. With the next series of three or four farts, titters begin to escape from mouths. The fifth or sixth fart evokes a flat-out laugh from a third of the audience. By the time the *sixteenth* fart rolls around, the entire audience is in a state of hysterical convulsion.'

BELOW: The Black sheriff of Rock Ridge (Cleavon Little, left) enlists the help of the Waco Kid (Gene Wilder, right).

ABOVE: As well as playing the governor, Mel Brooks also makes an appearance as a Sioux Indian chief in *Blazing Saddles*.

RIGHT: Bart (Cleavon Little, left) and his friend Charlie (Charlie McGregor, right) are up to their necks in trouble in *Blazing Saddles*.

BELOW: The new sheriff rides into Rock Ridge. From *Blazing Saddles*.

In *Blazing Saddles* Brooks has lassoed a whole corral load of western clichés and then sent them up unmercifully. The tone is set by Frankie Laine's lusty rendition of a title song that seems to make sense until you actually think about it ('He made his blazing saddle/A torch to light the way'). The joke here is twofold: on Frankie Laine's renown as the balladeer on classic westerns like *Gunfight at the OK Corral* (1957) and *3.10 to Yuma* (1957); and on the frequent banality and even stupidity of title song lyrics whose only function seems to be to publicize the film's title. (By a delicious irony, this naughty parody of the title song was nominated for an Oscar for 'best song.') Thereafter, the Wild West parody is mainly expressed through character. The Waco Kid (Gene Wilder) is a variation on the drunken gunman character who regains his self-respect, like Dean Martin in *Rio Bravo* (1959) or Lee Marvin in *Cat Ballou* (1965); and his fast draw – which is actually a brilliant visual cheat by director and editor – is straight out of the manual of *The Magnificent Seven* (1960). The saloon songbird Lili Von Shtupp (Madeline Kahn) is fast on the drawl, like Marlene Dietrich in *Destry Rides Again* (1939). The wretched townspeople in the church who anguish over what is to become of Rock Ridge now that people are being stampeded and cattle raped, recall the cowardly community of *High Noon* (1952), while some Mexican villains gleefully quote a line of their counterparts in *The Treasure of the Sierra Madre*, 'Badges? We don't need no stinking badges!'

There are numerous other references one could mention, but more important is the cumulative effect. It twists the traditional

western out of shape in order to show the deformity of some of the genre's values, notably the one about white supremacy. In its sympathy towards blacks and Indians, it assaults the western's notion of ethnic purity, a notion that has probably been taken to its extreme of neurosis by the John Wayne hero in Ford's *The Searchers* (1956). It is a defiantly 1970s' view of the western and its myths, very affectionate about some aspects (the heroism and adventurism) but also deeply suspicious of others (notably its paranoid racism). The film's insistence on the latter theme was probably influenced by Vietnam. Its depiction of the corrupt business and governmental organizations was no doubt influenced by Watergate. In his appearance as the governor, Mel Brooks even manages to look a bit like Richard

Nixon. The affection comes from Brooks's own love of westerns which in turn reflects his fondness for most aspects of mass entertainment. In its simultaneous evocation of America's pioneering past and its free allusions to other westerns that celebrate that heritage, *Blazing Saddles* anticipates a theme that was to be more thoroughly elaborated in Robert Altman's iconoclastic satire *Buffalo Bill and the Indians* (1976), namely, that the West represented not so much the heart of American adventurism but the origins of American showbiz.

One of Brooks's descriptions of *Blazing Saddles* was 'surrealist epic.' The epic nature of the film basically comes not from style but from theme, the birth of a nation. (Stylistically, the film turns the 1969 movie *The Wild Bunch* into The Crazy Gang and it

ABOVE: Bart takes himself prisoner to get out of a tight spot in *Blazing Saddles*.

RIGHT: Gene Wilder's alcoholic gunslinger, the Waco Kid, is a homage to Dean Martin's drunken deputy in *Rio Bravo*. Like Martin, Wilder's character will be redeemed by responsibility.

RIGHT: A toast to friendship: Gene Wilder (left) and Cleavon Little (right) in *Blazing Saddles*.

could be appropriately retitled *The Mirth of a Nation*.) The surrealism – of all his films this is probably closest to the lunatic license of a Spike Milligan or Monty Python – manifests itself in several ways. There are the anachronisms and gorgeous improbabilities, for example, whereby Nietzsche is cited amid the 'authentic frontier gibberish' of the church hall debate; where Count Basie appears in the desert to play 'April in Paris'; and where a handbill advertising jobs

for 'heartless villains' has the subtitle 'An equal opportunity employer.' In fact, the heartless villains who do apply for employment by Hedley Lamarr (Harvey Korman) burst the bounds of Wild West plausibility (anticipating the moment when the film will burst the bounds of the logic of its own setting) and become a comprehensive catalogue of Brooksian bad men – ranging from Nazis, Hell's Angels, Arabs through to the Ku Klux Klan.

LEFT: Cleavon Little as Bart in *Blazing Saddles*, a role originally intended for Richard Pryor.

BELOW: Partners in crime prevention: the Waco Kid and Sheriff Bart in *Blazing Saddles*.

RIGHT: Madeline Kahn plays the Teutonic songstress, Lili Von Shtupp in *Blazing Saddles*. Brooks has said that his original title for the film was: 'She Shtupps to Conquer.'

ABOVE: 'Is that a ten-gallon hat or are you just enjoying the show?' An enthralled audience watches Lili's routine in *Blazing Saddles*.

The hilarious absurdities accumulate. When the dumb but good-natured baddie Mongo (Alex Karras) thunders into town, he has 'Yes' and 'No' branded on the buttocks of his mule, like the 'love' and 'hate' signs tattooed on the fingers of Robert Mitchum's right hand and left hand respectively in Charles Laughton's superb thriller *The Night of the Hunter* (1955). (The music at this point brilliantly mimics the Mitchum theme.) Mongo is to become one of the sheriff's friends, but the characterization, unfortunately, was to cause Brooks considerable anguish when the parent of a handicapped child, believing the character's name to be Mongol, wrote to the *New York Times* complaining about Brooks's use of mental retardation as a subject for comedy. In his reply Brooks explained that Mongo was really intended as an affectionate spoof on the gentle giant character, Hoss, in *Bonanza*, played by Dan Blocker (to whom the film is dedicated). 'I must tell you, in all candor,' Brooks wrote in concluding his reply, 'reading that letter and the endorsement of it in the *Mental Retardation News* was one of the unhappiest moments of my life.'

Elsewhere, the humor is less controversial, just wild. The black sheriff (Cleavon Little) has to arrest himself in order to avoid an ugly mob. A fake town is constructed overnight to fool Slim Pickens's rampaging marauders. An old lady, being beaten up on the street, turns soulfully to the camera to say 'Have you ever seen such cruelty?' before returning to her beating; and as a man is being brutally pulled along the ground by a speeding horse he is heard to murmur, 'Well, that's the end of this suit.' Visual oddities include the shot of a man, about to be hanged, standing next to his horse which also has a noose round its neck;

ABOVE: Lili offers Bart some breakfast in *Blazing Saddles* after their night of love. Brooks's symbolism is not subtle but it does get its point across.

LEFT: An unusual backing group supports Lili's song 'I'm tired' in *Blazing Saddles*.

ABOVE: Olsen Johnson (David Huddleston) shows Lamarr's villainous poster to Bart and Waco in *Blazing Saddles*. Note the name of Huddleston's character: Olsen and Johnson were the comic team who headed the classic madcap comedy *Hellzapoppin* (1942), a big influence on Brooks's movie.

RIGHT: A replica of Rock Ridge is constructed to fool the villains in *Blazing Saddles*.

a tollgate in the wide open spaces for the Le Petomane Thruway that slows the progress of Pickens's gang; and a particularly significant detail where a black family has been so ostracized by the remainder of a wagon train that, when Indians attack, their wagon has to make its own circle.

This last example highlights the racial theme which is at the center of the film. All hellzapoppin is to break loose when the man appointed as sheriff of Rock Ridge is black. Prior to this event we have seen some neat mockery of black stereotypes, notably when black workers on a chain gang, taunted into singing a 'good old Nigger work-song,' are quite baffled by the cue of 'Swing low, sweet chariot' but do launch lustily into a swinging performance of 'I get a kick out of you.' But we have also seen the callous cruelty when handcart and workers are sucked into quicksand and it is the handcart that is to be rescued first. When black Bart arrives at the town to take up his new post, the people are so shocked that their 'Welcome Sheriff' sign rolls up in disgust of its own volition. Waco is to summarize for Bart the primitive qualities and attitudes of this typical western community: 'These people are simple farmers, people of the land, the common clay of the new West – you know, morons.' The development of the rest of the film is essentially devoted to the process whereby Bart will win them over and become as popular as Randolph Scott.

When he leaves, with a speech about stamping out injustice that strongly echoes Henry Fonda's final words in one of Brooks's favorite films, *The Grapes of Wrath* (1940), the townspeople will cry back affectionately, 'Bullshit!'

Blazing Saddles has a wide range of distinctive performances. Gene Wilder's characterization of Waco sees him at his most relaxed, mellow and charismatic while, in contrast, Harvey Korman as the corrupt Lamarr, on a 'great crusade to stamp out runaway decency in the West,' is all blustering bravura. Liam Dunn does a wonderful sub-Barry Fitzgerald impression of a cowardly cleric ('The time has come to

TOP: The raid on Rock Ridge in *Blazing Saddles*.

ABOVE: The town of Rock Ridge is plunged into chaos in *Blazing Saddles*.

TOP: Hedley Lamarr (Harvey Korman, left) consults the governor (Mel Brooks, center), with Miss Stein (Robyn Hilton, right) lending sympathetic support.

ABOVE: The fight for Rock Ridge spills over into the Warners' studio canteen in *Blazing Saddles*.

act and act fast – I'm leaving'); and Madeline Kahn's Teutonic Titwillow is pitched somewhere between Mae West ('Is that a ten-gallon hat or are you just enjoying the show?') and a lisping Lily Langtry. In her production number 'I'm Tired,' she does a brilliant pastiche of Marlene Dietrich's *Sprechstimme* drone and brings out all the ribaldry of a lyric whose argument seems to be that everything below the waist is a waste. *Blazing Saddles* is Madeline Kahn's first performance in a Mel Brooks film and she was to become a valuable member of the Brooks repertory, largely through her

gift at making sex funny – something which had escaped Brooks in *The Producers*.

Cleavon Little's performance as Bart is a little more contentious. Richard Pryor was originally cast and his manic manner might have been more stylistically appropriate. Nevertheless Little's gentleness is appealing and offers a respite from the relentless zaniness around him. Certainly his friendship with Waco – another of Brooks's buddy relationships – is sympathetically observed. A great flaw is Brooks's own performance as the governor, where he comes over as king of the leer but is nowhere near as funny as his performance as the rascally servant in *The Twelve Chairs*. Like *The Producers* too, *Blazing Saddles* rather runs down in the last ten minutes when the action bursts out of the western town and into a musical that is being shot on the adjoining lot. The film's games with movie myths and fantasies certainly allow for this flight of comic fancy, but the slapstick is relatively routine and over extended.

Overall, though, for its uninhibited sexual ribaldry and its raspberries at outmoded gallantry and heroism, *Blazing Saddles* was loved by audiences and was also nominated for Oscars (best song, best editing and Madeline Kahn as best supporting actress – all well deserved). To borrow the words of the title song, Brooks had conquered fear and he had conquered hate and, career-wise, he had turned dark night into day. For the remainder of the decade he was to go from strength to strength.

YOUNG FRANKENSTEIN

1974

RIGHT: Peter Boyle as the monster in *Young Frankenstein*.

BELOW: Frederick Frankenstein (Gene Wilder) drools over his alluring but demure fiancée, Elizabeth (Madeline Kahn).

Although the idea of *Young Frankenstein* apparently originated with Gene Wilder, Mel Brooks has said that he had been fascinated with the Frankenstein myth since childhood, particularly after seeing James Whale's classic 1931 film with Boris Karloff as the monster. In an interview on BBC television in 1986, Brooks could recall a childhood dream about the monster coming to get him on his Brooklyn fire-escape and waking up screaming 'The knobs! The knobs!' (In his film the monster has a zip-fastener rather than the traditional nut and bolt in his neck.) In this way the film

becomes a kind of exorcism. 'Maybe part of the reason for doing *Young Frankenstein*,' he said, 'was to make it terribly funny so I'd never have those dreams again.'

Since its publication in 1818 Mary Shelley's novel has never relinquished its grip on both the public and the critical imagination. The reason for this is its susceptibility to a wide range of interpretation and its seemingly limitless capacity to mold itself into a relevant shape for each succeeding age. In the Romantic age it was an extreme study of an individual whose genius isolates him from society. In a Victorian age increasingly riven by religious doubt, it became a cautionary tale of man's arrogance and of his desire to play God. In the post-nuclear age it became a text about the role and responsibility of science, with Dr Frankenstein a precursor of Oppenheimer, creating a monster (the bomb) over which he loses control. In the age of feminism it became a text about the arrogance of man who aspired to be not only God but woman, the story of a scientist who, envious of woman's creativity, creates his own baby. Persistently through the years, there has been a common confusion whereby Frankenstein has often been assumed to be the name of the monster whereas it is actually the name of the scientist who created him. This confusion has served to reinforce a major ambiguity in the novel: who is the real monster of the story?

Although *Young Frankenstein* is first and foremost a comedy, nearly all of the story's major themes – scientific ambition, the role of women, the tragedy of the monster – are touched on at some point in the film. In

many ways *Young Frankenstein* anticipates the Mel Brooks production of *The Elephant Man* (1980) which is also about a sensitive soul in a hideous body who is turned into a showbiz freak. Like Caliban in *The Tempest*, the monster has not been so brutalized by his captors that he cannot be moved by beauty, but his hideous appearance in society's eyes makes sympathy almost impossible (as the narrator in the novel puts it, 'I sometimes felt a wish to console him, but when I looked upon him . . .'). Interestingly, Brooks keeps in his film the important encounter between the monster and the blind man, who, because he cannot see the monster and therefore is not predisposed to fear him, treats him like a friend – or, as he puts it in the film, like 'an incredibly big mute.'

ABOVE: The sinister Frau Blücher (Cloris Leachman, right) is watched by the roving eye of Igor (Marty Feldman) as she threatens Frederick and Inga (Teri Garr) in *Young Frankenstein.*

RIGHT: Another, more genial 'monster': the hunchback Igor. One of the running jokes of the movie is the way Igor's hump moves from one shoulder to the other between different scenes.

46

BELOW: Frederick decides to search for Dr Frankenstein's secret laboratory.

The hero of *Young Frankenstein* is Dr Frankenstein's grandson Frederick (Gene Wilder) to whom we are introduced as he gives a scientific lecture and demonstration to eager students. It is clear he is sensitive about his heritage (he insists on being called 'Fronkensteen') but he also defends the scientific principles involved in the 're-animation of dead tissue' ('Look what has been done with hearts and kidneys,' he says.) This early scene prepares us for Frederick's ultimate attempts to resume his ancestor's experiments and bring a dead man back to life. It also prepares us for what Mel Brooks will do to *Frankenstein* – not so much parody it as perform a demented transplant on it.

'Pardon me boy, is this the Transylvania station?' Frederick inquires of a porter, who replies, 'Track 29.' Revisiting his grand-father's Transylvania home, Frederick will be greeted by a wild-eyed hunchback Igor, pronounced Eye-gor (Marty Feldman), a buxom serving maiden Inga (Teri Garr) and a sinister housekeeper Frau Blücher (Cloris Leachman), whose appearance prompts the horses to rear and causes them thereafter to whinny in terror whenever her name is even mentioned. Brooks here is exploiting the characterization of the original *Franken-stein* story, but he is also setting up a series of quite interesting character contrasts

RIGHT: Igor might have got hold of the wrong brain in *Young Frankenstein*.

BELOW: Frederick prepares to bring the monster (Peter Boyle) to life.

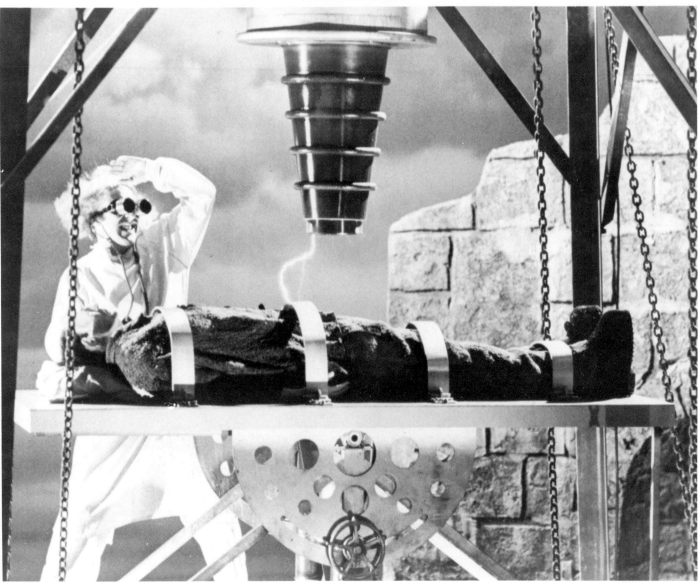

which will be developed later. The warm-blooded Inga contrasts with Frederick's frigid fiancée Elizabeth, delightfully played by Madeline Kahn in the register of a Geraldine Page spinster. Igor is a sort of trailer for the theme of the sensitive monster. He is so hideous that at one stage his mirror reflection frightens even himself. Yet he will not acknowledge his disability and is very proud. 'You know, I'm a rather brilliant surgeon, perhaps, I could help you with that hump,' says Frederick to him, to which Igor snaps back, testily, 'What hump?' End of conversation.

After Frederick has discovered his grand-father's secret laboratory and private library which conveniently has a copy of *How I Did It* by Victor Frankenstein, he and Igor steal a body from the graveyard and a brain from the brain depository. There are two problems, however. They are spotted at the graveyard by a constable and, in concealing the dead body under his coat, Frederick somehow contrives that the constable shakes hands with the corpse – one of a number of images that imply the dead hand of the past taking a grip on the living. Also Igor inadvertently chooses the brain not of a genius, but of a criminal, despite the bottles, as in James Whale's original, being clearly labelled (for example, 'Do not use this brain – Abnormal!').

Brooks is very like Whale in his stress on the technical paraphernalia of the experiment (the novel hardly mentions it). Frederick's speech about 'hurling the

BELOW: First steps: the monster meets his master.

ABOVE: The monster is cornered as Inga, Igor and Frederick look on.

gauntlet of science into the frightful face of death' eloquently expresses another theme of the novel to which Brooks deeply responds, the attempt of science to defeat death. The shadow grows on the wall as Frederick ascends, the shadow imagery being another recurrent visual motif in the film – perhaps to reflect the way the present is being shadowed by the past and to reflect the hero's attempt to give substance to the shadows of his creative imagination. 'Give

my creation life!' he cries – the cry of the scientist and the artist, through the ages – and with a crash of light, storm and wind, the experiment is launched and the monster infused with energy. 'It's alive!' they cry as the monster's hand at last begins to move and his fingers twitch. However, a portent of trouble is suggested when the monster's first action is an attempt to strangle his creator who, deprived of speech, has to act out the word 'sedative' to Inga and Igor and

actually stimulate her into a heartfelt vocal rendering of 'Ah, sweet mystery of life'; Frederick will become the husband of Inga; physical and psychological attributes will be transferred between creator and created. The monster will last be seen behind his copy of the *Wall Street Journal*; on her wedding night Inga will be heard to sing 'Ah, sweet mystery of life.'

Brooks extracts a lot of shameless humor in the film from sexual innuendo but a lot of the laughs understandably derive from genre recognition and a knowledge both of the Frankenstein myth and of former film styles. It was a brave decision to photograph it in black-and-white, but Gerald Hirschfield's glittering photography is superb and the sets and interiors stylishly designed and shot. Brooks makes use of old editing devices such as vertical and horizontal wipes to evoke the film-making style of an earlier period, and there is a particularly endearing heart-shaped iris shot after the monster and the maiden have made love and are now sharing their contented post-coital cigarette. The puns and running jokes so beloved of Brooks are as prolific and uneven as ever and the performances are effectively straight, against which the genre deformities and the situational

BELOW: 'This is a nice boy!' Frederick acknowledges his creation.

rely precariously on their expertise in interpreting charades.

The plot then develops along fairly traditional lines. The monster escapes; the townspeople are incensed; Frederick, at first appalled, gradually comes to acknowledge his own creation. In a series of twists toward the end, the monster will become romantically involved with Frederick's fiancée Elizabeth, whose fate worse than death at the hands of the monster will

RIGHT: A famous scene from the original *Frankenstein* (1931), with Boris Karloff as the monster playing with a little girl by a lake.

BELOW: Brooks's variation on the scene. The little girl (Anne Beesley) encounters Peter Boyle's monster.

absurdities effectively play. Gene Wilder's character genuinely develops and his acknowledgment of the monster is a full-blown emotional scene. 'This is a nice boy!' he exclaims as he embraces his creation, a favorite Brooks expression of understated passion. (Lily says the same about Bart in *Blazing Saddles* after their night of love and 'nice' is Max's description of his new receptionist in *The Producers* after she has left him slavering in sexual lust.) Madeline Kahn and Cloris Leachman are both very funny in their different ways and Peter Boyle's monster and Gene Hackman's blind man cameo are sensationally good.

Three scenes are as fine as anything that Brooks has directed. The first is the encounter between the escaping monster and the little girl who insists that he join her in her games. She throws flowers into the lake and then says, 'What shall we throw in now?' at which point the monster turns and looks craftily round at the camera. It is a moment in the film which particularly plays on our knowledge of James Whale's original, for in that film, Karloff's monster has thrown the girl into the lake expecting her to float like the flowers. The reference therefore adds both to the humor and the tension, as Brooks crosscuts the scene with one in which the parents first realize their girl is missing. However, when the girl asks the monster to 'sit down' on her seesaw and he heavily obliges, she is catapulted back through her bedroom window and onto her bed, at the moment the distraught parents open her door. The suspense and slapstick are superbly timed and the subversion of the original is done with deftness and charm.

The scene with the blind man is another classic of comic chaos and confusion. Overcome by his good fortune in discovering a friend the blind man turns on his hospitality. Inadvertently he pours soup in the monster's lap, shatters the monster's mug in a toast to 'long friendship,' and sets fire to the monster's thumb in an attempt to light his cigar. The monster rushes out before the coffee is served and the blind man is left shouting after him, 'I was going to make espresso!' It is a hilarious, painful, brilliantly acted little vignette about the difficulties of communication and the yawning gap between the kindly intentions of the heart and the clumsy inadequacies of the body. The blind man becomes almost an embodiment of Samuel Butler's choice little aphorism in his novel *The Way of All Flesh*, 'If it was not such an awful thing to say of anyone, I should say that he meant well.'

The other remarkable comic scene is the theatrical performance in which master and monster are now a double act, and the monster can embellish their routine with a strangulated interjection of 'Puttin' on the Ritz.' He has not simply been humanized but socialized, and here he is a parody of the sophisticated man about town. The film here is closest to Truffaut's *L'Enfant Sauvage* (1970) and its theme of civilizing

the wild, untamed spirit, which in turn will bring its own problems and discontents. Finally, however, Brooks's *Young Frankenstein* is an optimistic rendering of the myth, with the characters at the end achieving a marriage between the comforts of civilization and the vitality of the more instinctual, physical life. The monster will have a beneficial effect on the lives of the main characters – on their humanity, on their sexuality. By being on the monster's side Brooks plays fair with the original and is also true to his own deepest instincts, namely, a sympathy for the insulted and injured and oppressed.

BELOW: Misplaced kindness. The blind man (Gene Hackman) inadvertently pours hot soup into the monster's lap. From *Young Frankenstein*.

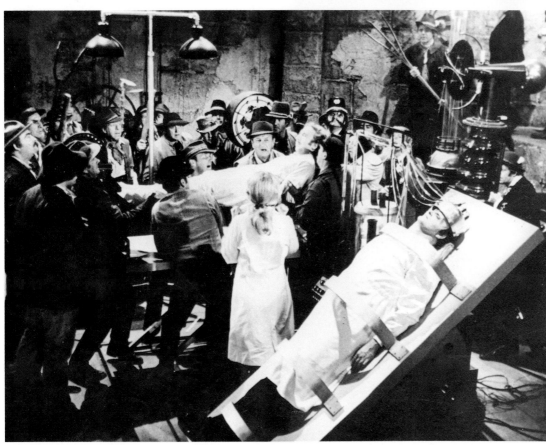

LEFT: Master, monster and mob in *Young Frankenstein*.

SILENT MOVIE

1976

RIGHT: Mel Funn (Mel Brooks) dreams up the idea of doing a silent movie.

BELOW: The three amigos: Dom DeLuise, Marty Feldman and Mel Brooks in *Silent Movie.*

Silent Movie is not a very silent movie. Can one imagine Mel Brooks being quiet for ninety minutes, if he were not actually asleep? What it does is attempt to revive the style of silent movies but within the context of contemporary movie technology. So, unlike *Young Frankenstein* which was shot in black-and-white, Brooks opts to shoot the film in color – a justifiable decision since the movie is not a period or stylistic reconstruction – and he has a score for full orchestra that responds very sensitively to the characters, the tempo and the mood.

Something should be said here about composer John Morris's consistently fine contributions to Mel Brooks's movies. The art of scoring for film comedy is easy to state but difficult to achieve. It calls on the composer to *augment* the film's humor and not simply alert an audience that this is intended to be funny. There is a good example of Morris's skill in *Silent Movie*. The music strikes up 'San Francisco/Open your Golden Gate' at an establishing shot of a big city skyline, and an audience instantly inwardly groans at the movie cliché. But wait . . . has the composer, as well as the audience, jumped the gun? There is a pause, a kind of silent clearing of the throat and the music now sheepishly corrects itself to the strains of 'Manhattan.'

The plot concerns a film director, Mel Funn (Brooks in his first starring role), down on his luck and with a drink problem, who hits on the idea of doing a silent comedy. Encouraged by his friends Marty Eggs (Marty Feldman) and Dom Bell (Dom De-Luise), he proposes the idea to his ailing studio boss (Sid Caesar) – 'I'm alright except for the constant pain' – whose Big Picture Studios are in danger of being taken over by a conglomerate called 'Engulf and Devour.' A deal is struck when the director per-suades a prestigious group of guest stars to participate in his movie, but tragedy almost strikes when Mel is vamped by a sexual siren (Bernadette Peters), who is first seen slipping out of a banana skin and who is secretly in the employ of Engulf and Devour. When he discovers her duplicity Mel starts hitting the bottle. However, all will be happily resolved.

As the above outline implies, *Silent Movie* is not all nostalgia and the plot has as much to say about modern Hollywood as the

RIGHT: Marty Feldman stars as Marty Eggs in *Silent Movie*.

BELOW: Dom DeLuise as Dom Bell in *Silent Movie*.

Hollywood of the past. Engulf & Devour are a brazen equivalent of the Gulf & Western company that took over Paramount. There is a fascinating account of this new atmosphere in a description of a Hollywood party in Robert Parrish's book *Growing Up in Hollywood*: the arrival of a Gulf & Western executive magnetizes the attention of all the male stars who cluster around him, leaving the ladies in the room unattended. As Parrish comments, there was a new lady in town. Brooks himself expressed his distaste for the conglomerate approach to cinema. He felt that an art was in danger of falling into the hands of uncaring businessmen, and that this made the task of the film-maker initiating his own project that much more difficult. (As he put it at the time, 'I made a deal with a group of people, not a building.') In *Silent Movie* Engulf and Devour are more interested in profit than in pictures and want to take over the studio in order to pull it down and set up a shopping mall. Brooks's contemptuous attitude to them is revealed in their literal worshipping of the dollar sign – for, in the Ben Hecht aphorism, 'in Hollywood, art is a synonym for bankruptcy' – and also by having Engulf (Harold Gould) when enraged, slaver like a rabid dog. (Ron Moody in *The Twelve Chairs* does the same when his character is at his most repulsive.)

Yet Mel Funn and Brooks to some degree do play the Engulf and Devour game. They both know that one way of getting a film off the ground is by packing it with stars, however incongruous. There is a marvelous, acid Billy Wilder anecdote about that aspect of modern Hollywood: A director goes to the Bank of America with a great story for a movie, asks for four million dollars, and is turned down because he does not yet know who is in it. Another director goes to the same people with a bag of horseshit, out of which he intends to make a picture, but with the names of Newman, Redford and Fonda raring to go – he is given the go-ahead and twelve million dollars. Never mind the quality, feel the stars. *Silent Movie* recognizes this reality. To its credit it also sends it up.

It sends it up by exaggerating the star persona of the celebrity whom Mel, Marty and Dom visit to cajole him or her into joining their movie. Burt Reynolds is all suavity and sexual narcissism. They appeal to him by massaging his ego as well as his hairy chest. James Caan appears as a punch-drunk boxer and all they have to do there is to reach down to his dumb decency. Paul Newman is convalescing from a racing

accident and in attempting to escape from them in his electric wheelchair, he enjoys the Keystone Cops chase so much that he thinks a movie in that vein might be fun.

LEFT: A typical *Variety* headline. From *Silent Movie*.

BELOW: Burt Reynolds (center) is joined in the shower by Dom Marty and Mel, who massage his chest and his ego.

ABOVE: Paul Newman is eager for a role in the silent movie after the thrill of a Keystone cops chase in a wheelchair.

RIGHT: Dom Bell (Dom DeLuise) gets caught up in the chase.

The elegant Anne Bancroft is approached in a Latin American night-club and won over through a combination of flattery and pratfalls, whereby the actress's relatively untapped comedy potential is shown in the deadpan dignity with which she endures violent humiliation. Mel sweeps her off her feet and cracks her head on a table in a frenzied tango worthy of Valentino. Marty draws out her latent talent for eyeball-rolling in a dexterous cross-eyed display in the manner of Ben Turpin or Eddie Cantor. Dom dazzles her with a fatso flamenco that succeeds in hammering the table through the floor.

The homely Liza Minnelli is persuaded when they turn up in the studio canteen as three tin men in armor (perhaps summoning up a wistful reminiscence of the Tin Man in her mother's 1939 classic *The Wizard of Oz*). They solicit her services in a gawky attempt at old-fashioned chivalry which is somewhat compromised when they inadvertently transfer some of her meal of grapes and cheese to her hair. The scene is this 'silent movie's' funniest use of sound –

clumsy courtship rendered through an extraordinary clanking cacophony. The movie's other major sound joke occurs when Marcel Marceau mimes a treacherous walk across a telephone wire in the wind to answer Mel's call; and, to the request to appear in the movie, the world's most famous mime utters the movie's one audible line of dialogue, *'Non!'*

One might think the absence of verbal humor would cramp Brooks's style. After all, one could not have too many jokes of the kind where the dialogue captions have clearly been censored and sanitized from the original statement, so that a mouthed 'son of a bitch' is tastefully transcribed as 'you're a bad boy.' However, Brooks was never worried about this. 'I've no patience for dialogue in the cinema,' he said in an interview in *Films and Filming.* 'Dialogue should be on the stage: action should be on the screen. I know that's stupid of me, but still I believe it – generally. When something talks too much, it's a play. When something moves a lot, it's a film.' Some of the visual jokes are in the old slapstick tradition, as

ABOVE: Mel Funn (Mel Brooks, right) demonstrates to Anne Bancroft that it takes two to tango.

LEFT: Dom (Dom DeLuise) performs a flabby flamenco in *Silent Movie.*

RIGHT: Three gay
caballeros: Dom, Mel and
Marty dance out their
desire for Anne Bancroft.

BELOW: Get well soon: Mel
and Dom prepare to visit
their studio chief in
hospital.

when Marty struggles to negotiate an
elevator; or when the 'torn from today's
headlines' urgency of the plot is conveyed
by newspapers being thrown from a passing
van with such velocity and ·regularity that

Liam Dunn's helpless news vendor eventually disappears under their bulk – a dis-
appearance that in turn becomes headline
news. (The joke was considered good
enough to be repeated, with very few
changes, in Amy Heckerling's 1984 comedy
Johnny Dangerously.) Brooks's favored
literal gags abound: audiences literally
sneak in to a sneak preview; when Mel has a
bright idea, a light bulb goes on above his
head. The best sight gag in the film is
literally the sickest, when the visitors get
involved in a game of video ping pong with
the studio boss's life-support machine.

As usual with Mel Brooks, one feels a real
affection for the world he is lampooning.
Silent Movie might be part of the modern
Hollywood where profit is god, more than
art or joy or entertainment, but it also
sincerely aims at giving you a good time. It
parodies the usual Hollywood-on-Holly-
wood plot. It exposes the harshness of the
community in the manner of *Sunset Boule-
vard* (1950); shows the importance of the
sneak preview as in *Singin' in the Rain*
(1952); and reworks the situation of the
drunkard trying to make a comeback as in

ABOVE: The sultry Vilma (Bernadette Peters) emerges out of a banana skin in *Silent Movie*. She is part of Engulf and Devour's plan to cause Mel to slip up.

LEFT: Vilma (Bernadette Peters) gets into her act.

A *Star is Born* (1954). However, everything is resolved happily. It is undeniably a genial entertainment and has a quality one does not normally associate with Brooks movies – charm. It is arguable, though, whether this is a strength or a weakness.

Silent Movie lacks the daring of *Blazing Saddles*, perhaps because Brooks is a little intimidated by the memory of the silent comedy masters of the past. It is easy to send up the western or the horror movie, however much you love them, but how do you send up Keaton or Chaplin, who were masters of self-satire? It lacks the density of *Young Frankenstein* because the characterization is so much more muted. The three main characters have attractive presences, with Brooks in his yachtsman outfit, Feldman as a cross-eyed pilot, DeLuise in a cultivated cashmere coat, but they seem to be rather short of comic business. DeLuise, in particular, who in *The Twelve Chairs* actually *started* at the end of his tether and then went farther and farther over the edge, is reined in here and, like Zero Mostel, he is a comedian who needs a berth as wide as his girth to enable him to show off his extraordinary gifts.

In general *Silent Movie* is a rather more inhibited Brooks film than usual, though typically, it celebrates and rewards the quality of innocence. The fans of his usual raucous raunchiness might be dismayed – like *The Twelve Chairs* this is a Mel Brooks movie for non-Mel Brooks lovers – but the restraint has its own rewards.

ABOVE: Marty and Dom watch anxiously as Vilma makes a vital phone call in *Silent Movie*.

RIGHT: A fallen Mel Funn (second from left) is revived by coffee and friendship in *Silent Movie*.

FAR RIGHT: Engulfed and devoured by true love: Vilma and Mel in *Silent Movie*.

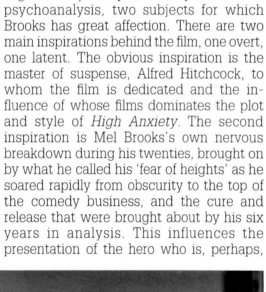

HIGH ANXIETY

1977

BELOW: Mel Brooks plays Dr
Richard H Thorndyke in
High Anxiety, a man with an
inexplicable and unnatural
fear of heights.

High Anxiety is a spoof on suspense and on psychoanalysis, two subjects for which Brooks has great affection. There are two main inspirations behind the film, one overt, one latent. The obvious inspiration is the master of suspense, Alfred Hitchcock, to whom the film is dedicated and the influence of whose films dominates the plot and style of *High Anxiety*. The second inspiration is Mel Brooks's own nervous breakdown during his twenties, brought on by what he called his 'fear of heights' as he soared rapidly from obscurity to the top of the comedy business, and the cure and release that were brought about by his six years in analysis. This influences the presentation of the hero who is, perhaps,

the most sympathetically drawn character in Brooks's entire work.

The plot concerns one Richard H Thorndyke (Mel Brooks) who has come to take over the top position of the psycho-neurotic Institute for the Very, Very Nervous. He is greeted with scarcely contained hostility by the assistant director, Dr Montague (Harvey Korman) and the head nurse, Miss Diesel (Cloris Leachman) but is delighted to find at the clinic his old teacher, Professor Lilloman (Howard Morris) who knows of Thorndyke's fear of heights. Thorndyke has been warned by his driver Brophy (Ron Carey) that his predecessor died in very mysterious circumstances. As Thorndyke slowly begins to unravel the mystery of the Institute and the truth about the former head's fate, in typical Hitchcock fashion he himself becomes the prey of the police and has to come to terms with his own psychological problems. But he secures the help of an ice-cool blond, Victoria (Madeline Kahn), worried about her father who is a patient at the clinic. Everything gathers toward a rousing climax in a bell tower where a traumatic flashback both explains and frees Thorndyke from his 'high anxiety.'

The narrative takes its basic shape from Hitchcock's *Spellbound* (1945) which concerns murder and trauma within the community of a psychiatric hospital, but the allusions to other Hitchcock movies as well are almost too numerous to catalogue. Thorndyke's fear of heights and the setting of the bell tower instantly recalls the James Stewart hero of *Vertigo* (1958), but falls from heights or threats, and fears of such falls recur in such Hitchcock movies as *Blackmail* (1929), *Rebecca* (1940), *Suspicion*

ABOVE: The poster for *High Anxiety*.

LEFT: Dr Thorndyke is welcomed to the Institute for the Very, Very Nervous by Dr Montague (Harvey Korman, second left) and Nurse Charlotte Diesel (Cloris Leachman, left).

RIGHT: Shock treatment: a patient is terrified by a vampiric Dr Montague while Thorndyke unsuspectingly tries to calm him down.

ABOVE: Nurse Diesel discloses a Nazi side to her nature.

mimicry inevitably extends to characterization. Nurse Diesel is an even more twisted symbol of compassionate service than Mrs Danvers in *Rebecca* while Victoria is one of those Grace Kelly-type heroines in Hitchcock whose cool exterior conceals flaming sexual passions. When Thorndyke calls her and is almost strangled as he tries to get through, she mistakes the caller for a heavy breather and is *definitely* interested.

As well as plot and character, equally important to the Hitchcockian ambience and to the humor of *High Anxiety* is the stylistic parody. The comedy, first of all, comes through recognition. When Thorndyke decides to have a shower we know we are in for a variation on the famous shower murder in *Psycho* (1960). The interest comes both from the incongruous imitation of the Hitchcock model (coy shots of Mel Brooks's nudity which is somewhat less erotic than Janet Leigh's) and from the variations. The assailant is not a deranged transvestite but a harassed bellboy (Barry Levinson) and the weapon is not a knife but a rolled-up newspaper. Brooks adds a touch of stylish homage. We see the black newsprint run down the sink. The film then cuts from the sink-hole to the hero's glazed eye, and finally Brooks caps the scene with a pay-off line, 'That kid gets no tip.' The second such scene occurs when Thorndyke

(1941), *Saboteur* (1942) and *North by Northwest* (1959). The stylistically frenzied final flashback, where the main character's obsession is shown to be rooted in childhood trauma, is similar to the revelations that conclude both *Spellbound* and *Marnie* (1964); and Montague's murder of an untrustworthy accomplice by tampering with his car recalls similar villainous malpractices in *Notorious* (1946), *North by Northwest* and *Family Plot* (1976). The

ABOVE: Hold the phone:
Thorndyke is attacked in a
phone booth by an assassin
(Rudy DeLuca).

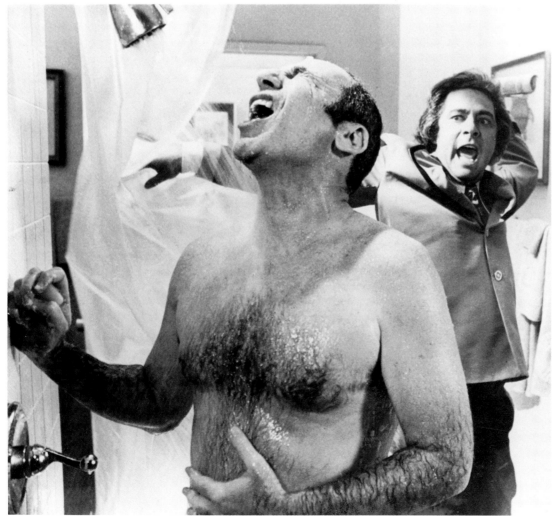

LEFT: Thorndyke is attacked
in the shower by an irate
bellboy (Barry Levinson)

RIGHT AND BELOW:
Thorndyke is splattered by
birds in *High Anxiety*. It is
an overt reference to the
Hitchcock film, *The Birds*,
in which our feathered
friends declared war on the
human race. Rod Taylor
(below) plays the
Hitchcock hero taking
evasive action.

agrees to meet Victoria at the North-by-
Northwest corner of the Golden Gate Park
and is not so much attacked as besplattered
by birds. (The simulated bird deposits were,
apparently, a mixture of mayonnaise and
chopped spinach.) Again the humor is en-
hanced by Brooks's precise stylistic mimicry: the birds gathering one by one behind
Thorndyke as they do in the schoolhouse
scene in *The Birds* (1963); the way they are
made to fly directly at the camera, as if we
too are in danger. It is the context that
makes this funny: the way Hitchcock's style
is being put to a comically incongruous use.

This is true not only of set-pieces but of
incidental detail. Just as Hitchcock liked the
kind of camera concentration that could
give him a close-up of a fingernail, Brooks
does an inconsequential huge close-up of

shadows around her provide an expressive image for a mind clouded by suspicions of her husband and for a character who feels like a fly caught in a trap. Hitchcock himself would have been proud of the way that scene proceeds into the next – a fade from the eyes of the nurse to the headlamps of the victim's car, as if the car has been given the evil eye. As soon as the windshield wipers are switched on to combat the rain we are in *Psycho* territory; the car as torture chamber.

Hitchcock's *emotional* use of color is scrupulously copied by Brooks. The color scheme for the lurid airport scene is predominantly red and orange; for the scenes at the hospital a metallic gray; and for the bird attack in the park a sickly green. John Morris's score is a splendid pastiche of Hitchcock's favorite composer, Bernard Herrmann, at his most incomparably agitated, though perhaps the best musical

BELOW: The lull after the storm: Thorndyke after the bird attack in *High Anxiety*.

Thorndyke's hand on an elevator rail when he is making his way through the airport. Thorndyke's vertiginous seizures are rendered in the form of a cartoon like the hero's nightmare in *Vertigo*. When Thorndyke is framed for a murder and has to run from the lobby of his San Francisco hotel, Brooks provides an aerial shot of his escape that recalls the shot of Thornhill's escape from the United Nations building in *North by Northwest*. When a nervous accomplice in *High Anxiety* says to Dr Montague, 'I feel like I'm caught in a web,' Brooks obliges by arranging web-shaped shadows on the wall behind him. This is not only a general reference to Hitchcock's use of Expressionist imagery to suggest emotional disturbance, it is a specific reference to a shot of Joan Fontaine in *Suspicion*: the web-like joke occurs when the driver tells Thorndyke about his predecessor and his suspicion of 'foul play!' The music suddenly strikes up in tension, but it turns out not to be Thorndyke's mood: it is the Los Angeles Philharmonic practicing in a coach that is travelling alongside his car.

Perhaps the most original aspect of Brooks's Hitchcockian homage is his use of the camera. The camera tracks slowly toward a window in a classic Hitchcock movement – and then there is a crash and the camera sheepishly retreats. It tensely follows Thorndyke's preparation for his shower – but then the lens starts misting up as the steam begins to gather. A tense conversation between Montague and Diesel is shot from beneath a glass-covered table, one of those crazy camera angles which Hitchcock loves to employ to increase tension (like the shots through the glass ceiling in his 1926 film *The Lodger* or the hugely ominous shot of the poisoned coffee cup in his 1946 thriller *Notorious*); but saucers, cups and trays contrive to obscure the camera's view of the action and it keeps having to adjust its position. As well as parodying Hitchcock's elaborate camerawork and his use of the camera to implicate an audience in his voyeuristic universe, Brooks does something quite unusual in screen comedy here – he makes the camera itself a comedian. Instead of simply recording the humor the camera moves about

ABOVE: James Stewart descends the staircase of the belltower in Hitchcock's *Vertigo*, the principal influence on *High Anxiety*.

RIGHT: Solving the crime, conquering his trauma: Thorndyke reaches the top of the belltower, helped by Victoria (Madeline Kahn).

idiosyncratically and this is often very comic in itself. It takes a really good comedy director to be able to use the camera not as the feed but as the funny man.

All this might make *High Anxiety* seem basically a game for Hitchcock aficionados, but there is more to it than that. The basic underlying joke of the film is that of an asylum where the doctors are clearly madder than the patients. The personnel includes a jailer with a half-mustache, a psychiatrist 'into' bondage and a nurse who likes dressing in Nazi uniform. 'You must remember we are dealing with dangerously sick people!' says Nurse Diesel, slamming a fork into the table. She is right up to a point. There is a patient who wanted to change the drapes in the Psychotic Game Room (the premise of Vincente Minnelli's 1955 psychiatrist melodrama *The Cobweb* known in the trade as 'The Drapes of Wrath'); a greeting from the Violent Ward consists of a rock lobbed through the new doctor's window. Mainly Thorndyke has more to fear from his colleagues and the film becomes a comedy concerned with the relativity of madness – it's a mad, mad, mad, mad world.

The two funniest scenes of *High Anxiety* are also probably its most important. Thorndyke and Victoria, in order to get through airport security, hit on the idea of disguising themselves as an obnoxious, quarrelling Jewish couple and are ushered through with some haste. 'If you're loud and annoying,' explains Thorndyke, 'psychologically people don't notice you.' Again it is a neat variation of a Hitchcockian device where a hero often has to get himself out of a tight spot by drawing attention to himself, like the scene in *North by Northwest* where Cary Grant disrupts an auction in order to avoid James Mason's thugs, or the one in *Torn Curtain* (1966) where Paul Newman panics a theater audience by shouting 'Fire!' in order to avoid capture by the encircling East German police. The line might even be Brooks's own embittered comment on the critical reception of his own movies. 'A small thing, but annoying,' said the critic Philip French about the misspelling of 'Piccadilly' in *To Be Or Not To Be* (1983) and then added, 'like Brooks himself.' Because he has been loud and 'annoying,' critics and the industry have not given him or his

ABOVE: Thorndyke prepares to climb the staircase, against the protestations of the beautiful blond, Victoria. The driver Brophy (Ron Carey) and Professor Lilloman (Howard Morris) watch with great anxiety.

ABOVE: 'If you're loud and annoying, psychologically people don't notice you.' A disguised Thorndyke in *High Anxiety*.

collaborators the credit he feels they all deserve, something which clearly still rankles.

The comic highlight of the film, though, is Thorndyke's unexpected rendering of the title song 'High Anxiety' in the hotel bar. It is a lovely dig at the inanity of so many film title songs, with Brooks once again revealing a gift as lyricist that puts him roughly midway between the polished wit of a Sondheim and the inspired nonsense of an Ogden Nash. It is also genuinely charming. Brooks does a superb vocal impression of Frank Sinatra, imitating Sinatra's odd phrasing and his habit of fracturing lyrics into idiosyncratic, not to say meaningless, syllables ('ang-*ziety* . . . oo-ziety'). As the song develops, so does the confidence of the vocalist. He executes a little run up the orchestra steps, confidently pulls around the microphone lead, and at one moment cracks it like a whip, producing an excited reaction in Victoria (another hint that her frigid facade might be deceptive).

The scene is so good because it is not simply Mel Brooks having a good time but the moment when the harassed and persecuted Thorndyke suddenly blossoms into the romantic hero of his dreams. Hitchcock's films have often been read as a

RIGHT: Victoria and Thorndyke evade detention at the airport by disguising themselves as a quarrelsome Jewish couple whom no one would wish to detain.

We learn at the end that Thorndyke's fear of heights stems from a childhood incident when he fell out of his high-chair during a family quarrel. Because his parents have *not* been good to him Thorndyke has been traumatized. His little speech at the end of his song is a little idealistic prayer, an appropriate final flourish for an episode of wish-fulfillment in the hero's life.

As *High Anxiety* develops, it becomes clear that most of the adults in the movie have never matured or grown up. This is particularly emphasized in the scene when Thorndyke gives a lecture on 'penis envy.' The discussion which follows linguistically disintegrates when a visitor brings two young girls into the lecture theater for, in their embarrassment and their attempt to find alternatives for the 'naughty words,' the psychiatrists wind up looking more childish than the children. *High Anxiety* is about retarded development, a theme seen in both comic and compassionate terms and if the film is more affecting and less aggressive than the usual Brooks, the reason perhaps has something to do with his identification with the vulnerability of Thorndyke and his affection for his child-like innocence. Beneath the Hitchcock paraphernalia beats one of Brooks's most personal films – and one of his best.

ABOVE: Thorndyke is framed for murder in *High Anxiety*, a scene reminiscent of the United Nations murder in Hitchcock's *North by Northwest*.

LEFT: Romantic hero: Mel Brooks in *High Anxiety*.

projection of his own romantic fantasies and in this scene Brooks is doing a similar thing. Also Thorndyke's signing-off tag at the end of his song ('And remember folks, be good to your parents – they've been good to you') is not only a joke at the expense of the specious moralizing of the popular song, but it alludes to an important theme of the film.

HISTORY OF THE WORLD – PART I

1981

It was perhaps inevitable that Mel Brooks's 2000-Year-Old Man would inspire his creator to give some thought to the whole development of the human race over the centuries. This film is, in part, the result of that. However, it is not simply a history of the world, it is also an anthology of the bad joke (from satirical to scatological, from innuendo to anachronism) and also an amused homage to the way the film world has represented the past on screen. The manner of the film refers to the work of Cecil B De Mille and D W Griffith but, in Brooks's words, 'only in terms of capturing the grand scale of human behavior stylistically on film.' Indeed, the film is more influenced by the manner of Richard Lester in such films as *A Funny Thing Happened on the Way to the Forum* (1966) and *The Three Musketeers* (1973). The modern perspective

BELOW: The Dawn of Man as portrayed in *History of the World – Part I.*

on history in these movies not only satirizes the past but suggests a continuity with the present, recognizing that these too were periods of inequality, injustice and confusion and that people through the ages have responded to adversity with similar kinds of stoicism or desperation. As Brooks put it, 'My job as a comedy film-maker is to point out and remind us of what we are – to humble us and expose our foibles.'

The film had Brooks's biggest budget up to that date. Richard Pryor had to be dropped from the cast when he had his much-publicized burning accident and he was replaced by Gregory Hines. Brooks has five roles (as he says in the French Revolution episode, 'It's good to be the king') and at least that many plots, for this is his most episodic work. It is not so much a narrative as variations on a theme. He might have been influenced in his choice of structure by Woody Allen's *Everything You Always Wanted to Know About Sex But Were Afraid to Ask* (1972), which is similarly constructed, or the Monty Python movies like *Life of Brian* (1979) which make a virtue out of discontinuity; or it might have been his response to the common criticism of his films that they break down into inspired episodes more than involving plots and that the parts seem greater than the whole. Why not make a film that is frankly made up of episodes, but is held together by a dominant theme? That theme is not simply the history of the world, but the cruelty and injustice of that history.

In the opening 'Dawn of Man' sequence Brooks briskly covers such momentous discoveries as fire and the spear, laughter and music, and man's need to create and

procreate. Mock solemnity is conferred on these proceedings by Orson Welles's grandiloquent narration and by the use of Richard Strauss's opening to his symphonic poem *Also sprach Zarathustra* which Stanley Kubrick used so impressively for his 'Dawn of Man' sequence in *2001: A Space Odyssey* (1968). Yet this paradise of human potential is not without its darker side. The birth of the artist is followed immediately by the birth of the critic who 'pisses' on the artist's creation (one can hardly avoid seeing Brooks's own bitterness in that). Music is born when a brick is dropped on someone's toe and rhythmically organized pain along these lines rapidly leads to the composition and performance of the 'Hallelujah Chorus' from Handel's *Messiah*. This small episode brings to the fore two essential elements in the humor of the film: pain (for Brooks's history of the world contains little else) and blasphemy (which will sometimes take the film quite close to the wicked surrealist wit of the great Spanish director, Luis Buñuel). The element of blasphemy is carried over into Brooks's superb Old

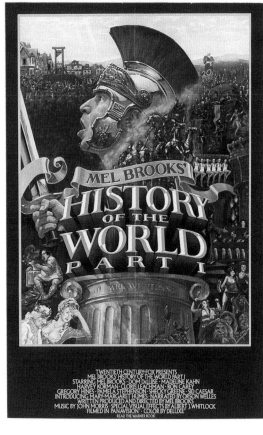

ABOVE: Mel Brooks as Moses, unfortunately dropping one of the tablets of stone, thereby reducing Fifteen Commandments to Ten.

LEFT: The poster for *History of the World – Part I*.

ABOVE: Mel Brooks at the original Caesar's Palace.

RIGHT: Dom DeLuise as the Emperor Nero.

Testament joke where Moses, rather brow-beaten by God, is tempted to take evasive action ('I hear you, I hear you, a deaf man could hear you . . .') and then drops one of the tablets of stone, so that Fifteen Commandments are reduced to Ten. If Brooks is remembered for nothing else, he should be remembered for his wonderfully simple explanation for human imperfection, that some of the Commandments got broken during transportation.

In the 'Roman Empire' episode, the main characters are a philosopher Comicus (Mel Brooks) and a black slave (Gregory Hines) and we follow their adventures in a comic-ally evoked Ancient Rome. An opening panning shot reveals a market complete with soothsayers, plumbing salesmen, and a stall for used chariots. At the unemploy-ment exchange an out-of-work gladiator is being interviewed: 'Did you kill last week? Did you try to kill last week?' When Comicus describes his former philosophical employment as the coalescence of the 'vapor of human behavior into logical com-prehension' the interviewer responds by

LEFT: The Empress Nympho (Madeline Kahn) selects escorts for a forthcoming orgy in *History of the World – Part I*.

BELOW: A chariot chase in *History of the World – Part I*. Brooks is in the driving seat: also aboard are Mary Margaret Humes and Gregory Hines.

summarizing briskly, 'O, a bullshit artist.'

Comicus is later to perform a stand-up comic routine at Caesar's Palace before the Emperor Nero (Dom DeLuise at his most fulsome and flatulent). His Christian jokes go down well ('They're so poor, they only have *one* God'). However, he flounders when the jokes stray onto the sensitive subjects of obesity and the corruption of the Roman Senate and he is led away muttering, 'When you die at the Palace, you really *die* at the Palace.' He will have to fight his black friend at a gladiators' arena in a scene that alludes to a similar development in Kubrick's *Spartacus* (1960), but they will escape in a chase scene in which white horses outrun black, that refers to the chariot race in Wyler's *Ben-Hur* (1959).

Rather like the script for *A Funny Thing Happened on the Way to the Forum*, Brooks piles in all the Ancient Roman jokes he can think of, from vestal virgins with 'No Entry' signs to outrageous puns (such as Nero's request, 'Bring me a small lyre,' at which point a little man is dragged in, repeating 'I didn't do it, I didn't do it . . .') Because *Forum* covered the humorous potential of Roman-ness so thoroughly, Brooks's version looks a bit repetitive and faded. His reference to the Romans' 'wine break' cannot really stand comparison with the wine joke of *Forum*, 'Was One a good year?'

Curiously, though, wine is the factor that leads to another of the best inspirations of

ABOVE: The Last Supper, with John Hurt (center) as Christ, and a guest appearance by the wine waiter (Mel Brooks).

RIGHT: 'The Inquisition – what a show!' Mel Brooks leads the dance.

the film, when Comicus is employed as wine waiter at the Last Supper. His cross-talk with John Hurt's Christ, where the former's expletive ('Jesus!') confuses the latter who believes he is being addressed in person ('What?'), is not terribly funny, yet it does further the blasphemy theme and it does prepare for the moment when Leonardo's 'group portrait' of the Last Supper has Comicus appearing behind the head of Christ like a halo. (As with the use of the 'Hallelujah Chorus' in an irreligious context, this is another reference to Buñuel's 1961 masterpiece *Viridiana* which also restages

and then freezes the Last Supper in a startlingly incongruous way.) The main humor of the scene, however, comes from the contrast between the traditional religious piety associated with the scene and the rude human practicality which would have occurred to hardly anyone but Mel Brooks. For example, how many at the supper wanted soup and were they intending to pay singly or together?

If 'The Last Supper' sequence borders on tastelessness, Brooks's following sequence positively embraces it. The Spanish Inquisition is rendered as an elaborate production

number, which includes heads used as bongos and prisoners' knees used for a xylophone cadenza. Mel Brooks stars as the Grand Inquisitor, doing a spectacular musical comedy slide as the song tempo picks up; a Jewish prisoner mimics Rex Harrison's song delivery style in *My Fair Lady*; and nuns strip off their habits to become an instant Busby Berkeley chorus line. 'The Inquisition – what a show!' sings the chorus. It is probably Brooks's most elaborate musical number since 'Springtime for Hitler' in *The Producers* and it works on the same principle of counterpoint – the cheerfulness of the music against the horror of the torture theme, with the intention of making oppression look ridiculous. The concept is debatably dubious but the execution is undeniably dazzling.

The weakest section of the film, 'The French Revolution,' is unfortunately also the last and the longest. The problem again is the staleness of some of the jokes – of the 'the peasants are revolting' category – and the fact that both the humor and the harshness have been done better in Lester's *The Three Musketeers*. Like Lester, Brooks is attentive to the inequalities of French society, with apple cores and dead rats being offered for sale as food, though he seems no more sympathetic to revolution as a solution to human ills than he did in *The*

Twelve Chairs. As in the Lester film, Spike Milligan makes a startling guest appearance as a filthy prisoner, causing a cloud of dust to rise from his shirt when he strikes his heart and commanding his caged canaries to 'fly' in celebration of their freedom, at which point they promptly drop down dead. Also like the Lester film, there is a royal chess game with live chess pieces (in *Musketeers* they are dogs, in the Brooks film they are commoners).

TOP: A medieval chorus line from *History of the World – Part I*.

ABOVE: A change of habit: nuns miraculously transform themselves into Busby Berkeley bathers.

ABOVE: To the rescue: Mademoiselle Rimbaud (Pamela Stephenson) and her father (Spike Milligan) are defended by the king – or is it the 'piss bucket' boy Jacques?

Mel Brooks plays a dual role – as the 'piss' bucket boy (a fleeting recollection of Brooks's portrayal of the birth of criticism at the beginning of the film) and as the king, whose idea of game hunting is to shoot a peasant from out of the sky (again a kind of visual pun reminiscent of that moment in Lester's 1959 short *The Running, Jumping and Standing Still Film* when we have a shot of a shot putter's shot being shot out of the sky). With his short mustache, Brooks as the king looks a little like Chaplin and the plot has elements of *The Great Dictator* (1940) with physically identical men at either end of the social hierarchy being drawn into ever closer plot proximity. Mistaken for the king by the revolting peasants and about to be guillotined, Brooks's commoner is rescued when the horse, Miracle, ridden by Gregory Hines, comes thundering in from the Roman Empire section to whisk him to safety. 'How did you do it?' asks Brooks. 'Movies is magic,' explains Hines. It is an ending of joyous artificiality in the manner of the *Blazing Saddles* finale, breaking both the rules and the bounds of conventional screen comedy.

Two quotations spring to mind when thinking of *History of the World – Part I*. The first is that comment by Alec Guinness's cleric about his west window in Robert Hamer's classic black comedy *Kind Hearts and Coronets* (1949), 'it has all the exuberance of Chaucer without, happily, any of the concomitant crudities of his period.' Brooks has all the exuberance of Chaucer and sometimes happily, sometimes unhappily, also *all* the concomitant crudities. The second is Dickens's opening to *A Tale of Two Cities*: 'It was the best of times, it was the worst of times . . . .' *History of the World* is the best of Brooks and it is the worst of Brooks. At its best – with Brooks as Moses, or serving at the Last Supper, or dancing at the Spanish Inquisition – we see a comedian whose inventiveness, originality and imagination can give new heights to comic outrageousness. At its worst – with the relentless puns, the unfunny gay jokes, the lack of narrative drive, the tenuous structure – the sound that arises is not helpless laughter but the dull flogging of a dead horse. Yet Brooks has one more joke up his sleeve. An end-title has a brief trailer for Part II. Highlights will include Hitler on Ice, A Viking Funeral and an episode entitled 'Jesus in Space' with a lunar module shaped like a Star of David. Again this trailer might be an allusion to Lester's *The Three Musketeers* which also ends with a montage of a forthcoming sequel. But it is also a bluff: Brooks has no such sequel in mind; in *History of the World – Part I* he was merely parodying Hollywood mannerisms.

LEFT: 'It's good being the king': Louis XVI (Mel Brooks) has his pick of female companions.

BELOW: Waiting for the end: the king's look-alike, Jacques (Mel Brooks) prepares to meet his doom.

TO BE OR NOT TO BE

1983

RIGHT: Anne Bancroft plays Anna Bronski, the old Carole Lombard role, in the remake of *To Be Or Not To Be*.

BELOW: A typical Mel Brooks production number from *To Be Or Not To Be*.

FACING PAGE TOP: Mel Brooks and Anne Bancroft in *To Be Or Not To Be*, playing a husband and wife team.

FACING PAGE BELOW: The Bronskis acknowledge the applause for their Polish version of 'Sweet Georgia Brown.'

Like Woody Allen with *Play It Again, Sam* (1972) which was directed by Herbert Ross, Mel Brooks took a break from direction in *To Be Or Not To Be*. He handed over the reins to a trusted colleague, Alan Johnson, who had been choreographer and associate producer on previous Mel Brooks movies. Perhaps Mel felt he needed a change, but it is more likely that he realized he would have to give all his concentration to his perform-ance. For in this film he plays three of the most challenging roles of his, or any other actor's career – Hamlet, Hitler and himself.

Brooks plays an actor-manager Bronski who is 'world famous in Poland.' He is so egomaniacal that he regards World War II as an unpardonable interruption of his theatri-cal career. He is also so vain that his wife Anna (Anne Bancroft) who acts with him has to suffer the indignity of seeing her

name placed on the bill poster within paren-theses. Unkind critics have seen a bio-graphical parallel in this. When Mel Brooks is in full flight, nearly everyone around him, so to speak, is placed in parentheses.

Nevertheless the Brooks-Bancroft duo in *To Be Or Not To Be* has a good deal of charm. Also Bronski's narcissism and arrogance are either punctured or satirized through the film, which turns the joke good-naturedly on Bronski/Brooks himself. There is a running joke of a young flyer (Tim Matheson) who always walks out when Bronski begins Hamlet's 'To be or not to be' soliloquy: he is actually stealing backstage to see Anna, but Bronski is more offended at

the insult to his performance than at the possibility of infidelity. Later Bronski has to impersonate a Nazi in order to protect a member of the Polish underground. It is a brave and hazardous gesture, but his first thought following the success of his mission is to ruminate rather sadly that, 'I gave the greatest performance of my life – and nobody saw it.'

The film is a remake of the 1942 Ernst Lubitsch classic of the same name. Lubitsch said that one of the attractions of the material for him was its affectionate satire of the vulnerable vanity of actors – a theme that the Brooks film also retains. ('You parachuted into Poland just to see me?' says Anna to the flyer who is actually trying to contact the Polish underground about the imminent arrival of a traitor in their midst.) However, the real force of the original comes from its satire on what Lubitsch called the 'ridiculous ideology of Nazism.' As we have seen, in this respect it is an important precursor of Brooks's *The Producers*. Curiously it was the one film of Lubitsch that ran into the kinds of accusations of bad taste that have persistently pursued Brooks. Critics complained about what they called 'a callous, tasteless effort

to find fun in the bombing of Warsaw.' A joke by the Nazi Colonel Erhardt about the leading character's acting – 'What he did to *Hamlet*, we are doing to Poland' – was particularly thought to cross the border from comedy to cruelty. In fact, what Lubitsch was doing was exactly what Brooks has always sought to do: bringing abhorrent views out into the light in order to pour witty and withering scorn upon them.

Nevertheless there are considerable differences in the Lubitsch and the Brooks approach to comedy. There has been some dispute over the effectiveness of the remake and whether the styles of two such comic originals can really be meshed. *To Be Or Not To Be* is undoubtedly the most subdued and plot-oriented film in which Brooks has been involved, even seeming to simplify the original plot which, as Truffaut observed, defies summary or analysis an hour after you have seen the film. (Truffaut, incidentally, had made his own homage to the Lubitsch film in his 1980 drama about the Occupation and theatrical intrigue, *The Last Metro*.) For some critics, the more orthodox narrative structure was a welcome infusion of discipline into Brooks's usually disorderly conduct. Also the visual style was modest to the point of self-effacement. In fact, some of the compositions are virtual replicas of shots in the Lubitsch film (for example, the camera set-up when Bronski, about to meet with the spy Siletski, is advised by his compatriots not to overplay his part as 'Concentration Camp' Erhardt). But is this discipline and homage, or more like timidity and caution?

The problem with the remake is that it is

ABOVE: Mel Brooks at last gets a chance to impersonate Hitler.

RIGHT: 'Heil myself': Bronski (Mel Brooks) satirizes Hitler in a theatrical revue in *To Be Or Not To Be*.

ABOVE: Siletski (José Ferrer, left) suspects that Colonel Erhardt is not what he seems — as indeed he is not.

SECOND LEFT: Bronski explains to his wife that Hamlet's most famous soliloquy has resulted in an unexpected walk-out.

LEFT: Mel Brooks as Hamlet.

more of a copy of a classic than a reviatalization of that classic's themes. Inevitably, it lacks the original's urgency which came quite naturally out of the fraught war-time period in which it was being made, a time when the outcome of the war was still in doubt. In the remake even the period reconstruction seems half-hearted. In some ways the film seems less about the theater or about fascism than about Mel Brooks himself: the comic who wanted to play Hamlet *and* Hitler and at last gets the chance to do so in the same film.

Brooks does attempt to do a character

ABOVE: Siletski (Jose Ferrer, left) suspects that Colonel Erhardt is not what he seems — as indeed he is not.

SECOND LEFT: Bronski explains to his wife that Hamlet's most famous soliloquy has resulted in an unexpected walk-out.

LEFT: Mel Brooks as Hamlet.

RIGHT: Sasha (James Haake, left), Anna (Anne Bancroft, center) and Bronski bid farewell to their home, now occupied by the Nazis.

BELOW: The Polish flyer, Sobinski (Tim Matheson, right) endeavors to involve the Bronskis in his attempt to contact the Polish underground about the traitor in their midst.

performance as Bronski and at least offers a fresh approach. Whereas Jack Benny's actor-hero in the Lubitsch original breathed an aristocratic arrogance, Brooks substitutes his own brand of nervous aggression. Yet his admiration for Lubitsch cannot conceal a world of difference between Lubitsch's essentially European sophistication and Brooks's essentially Jewish bellicose broadness. Brooks's inevitable musical routines – a Polish version of 'Sweet

Georgia Brown,' a production number that improbably rhymes 'ladies' with 'Hades,' a Hitler showstopper about the Führer's desire for peace ('a little piece of Poland, a little piece of France, a little slice of Turkey) – will seem coarse-grained for those who remember the suave wit of the original. On the other hand, for Mel Brooks fans these numbers will seem the highlight of the film. They might also seem underdeveloped in comparison with a number like 'Springtime for Hitler' and a reminder of the outrageous wit of which Brooks is capable but which in this film is strangely subdued. The impression throughout is of Brooks on a leash. This still means that he is often more manic than most, but he never touches his higher flights of lunacy.

There are some good supporting performances. In the old Carole Lombard role, Anne Bancroft reveals a genuine gift for comedy which the movie industry has only rarely exploited. When her husband is forbidden to play Hitler for fear it might give offense and has to play Hamlet instead, she comments, ruefully, 'And that's *not* offensive?' Like Lombard, Bancroft has an infectious naughtiness in the role ('True love should never stand in the way of a good time!') Equally good is Charles Durning's Oscar-nominated performance as Erhardt which wisely makes no attempt to copy the incomparable Sig Ruhmann in the original,

LEFT: 'Ladies': Bronski is surrounded by beautiful girls in an elaborate musical number.

BELOW: The theater of war: Bronski's theatrical troupe under threat in *To Be Or Not To Be*.

ABOVE: Sasha and Anna are harassed by Nazis.

RIGHT: A fake professor (Mel Brooks) and a Nazi colonel (Charles Durning) are equally bemused by the bewildering turn of events in *To Be Or Not To Be*.

but instead displays a conscientious characterization which allows the comedy to emerge naturally out of the situation. He is excellently supported by Christopher Lloyd as his hapless adjutant Schultz. The performances of Tim Matheson as the flyer and José Ferrer as the traitor are certainly not inferior to the corresponding performances in the original. It is not as well cast in the supporting roles as the Lubitsch, and the gay dresser (James Haake) is a conces-

sion to modern tastes of humor that, for all the skill of the performance, rather jars against the 1940s' background. Authenticity is something of a problem for the film, which it does, however, acknowledge quite amusingly when the incomprehensible opening dialogue is interrupted by a Cecil B De Mille-type voice from on high proclaiming, 'In the interests of clarity and sanity, the rest of the movie is not in Polish. . . .'

Overall it is a genial entertainment, but

the total effect is a bit tepid and (dare one say this of a Mel Brooks film?) excessively tasteful. Stripped of the immediacy of the context, it has none of the risk of the original. Also Lubitsch's film had a bleak visual claustrophobia that counterpointed the comedy and appropriately recalled the paranoid atmosphere of the anti-Nazi melodramas of Fritz Lang. This new version is in rather bland color which contributes little to the dramatic or comic impact.

It has all the ingredients of a characteristic Mel Brooks film – the anti-Nazi theme, the daringly dubious comedy, the theatrical background, a plot of doubles and disguise. What is missing is the usual boisterous sparkle and, surprisingly, the usual intermittent tone of tenderness: it is all a little flat and cold. It seems more a remembrance of things past than a freshly inspired rollicking romp. Unlike Woody Allen who can occasionally become Ingmar Bergman, Mel Brooks can only really be himself. Uneasy lies his head when he has to wear Ernst Lubitsch's crown. Something of that uneasiness is disclosed in a comment of Bronski himself when he has to assume another person's identity and is told that 'you'll make a better Siletski than Siletski.' 'I hope so,' he replies 'he's dead.'

BELOW: A confrontation with the Führer. Having first played Hamlet, Bronski must now play Hitler.

LEFT: Stage Nazis in a deadly game. Bronski's theatrical troupe, posing as German officers, become implicated in the killing of a Nazi spy. From left to right, George Gaynes, Mel Brooks, Zale Kessler, Lewis J Stadlen, Jack Riley and George Wyner.

CONCLUSION

In the 1971 *Action* interview, Brooks lists two of his favorite films as Ford's *The Grapes of Wrath* (1940) and Jean Renoir's *La Grande Illusion* (1937) – neither of them, as he concedes, 'a flat-out laff riot.' This might imply that way deep down he is yet another comedian with a yearning to play Hamlet, which *To Be Or Not To Be* barely satisfied. Might it be that the commercial failure of *The Twelve Chairs* – which, for all its

BELOW: Mel Brooks poses with Pamela Stephenson, who co-starred with him in *History of the World – Part I.*

humor, is the most overtly serious and moralistic of his movies – is the only thing that has discouraged Brooks from going farther down that dramatic road?

Actually, that is unlikely. It seems that he has never been tempted to be straight-faced about the weighty subjects he has treated comically. Unlike Woody Allen, Mel Brooks has never wished to make his *Interiors*. 'Why should I indulge myself,' he remarked in an interview in *Films and Filming*, 'and do a David Lean-ish kind of film – which I *could* do – not as well as David Lean can but you know what I mean. I could do my little Jewish *Brief Encounter* and disguise it – shorten the noses. But it wouldn't be as much fun as my delivering my dish of insanity. That's what I'm good at. That's what I can do.'

In recent years this question has received an added twist with the formation of his own production company, Brooksfilms, which has made films significantly different from Mel Brooks's own, yet having quite an interesting relationship with those that Brooks has directed. For example, Brooksfilms productions such as David Lynch's *The Elephant Man* and David Cronenberg's *The Fly* (1986) both share an important theme with *Young Frankenstein*: the tragedy of a hero with human feelings trapped inside a grotesque physical frame. Whereas Brooks's own movies are comedies of deformity of various kinds (deformity of genres, or stereotypes, or attitudes), these productions are tragedies *about* deformity. One even wonders if they are some kind of compensation for the controversy mentioned earlier about the characterization of Mongo in *Blazing Saddles* which

ABOVE: Marty Feldman in a tight spot in his film, *The Last Remake of Beau Geste*. Feldman was one of a number of Brooks's performers who was encouraged to turn his hand to direction.

LEFT: Freddie Jones plays an unscrupulous fairground operator in *The Elephant Man*, a Brooks-films production whose seriousness and sensitivity took critics by surprise.

TOP: Sigerson Holmes (Gene Wilder, second right) apprehends Moriarty (Leo McKern, right) in *The Adventures of Sherlock Holmes' Smarter Brother.*

ABOVE: Marty Feldman (left) in *The Adventures of Sherlock Holmes' Smarter Brother.* Here he arrests Moriarty's messenger Finney (Roy Kinnear).

upset Brooks so deeply. Yet these productions also testify to Brooks's shrewd film sense. In both cases, the choice of director was risky – Lynch only being known for his sickly, surreal horror movie *Eraserhead* (1976), Cronenberg being notorious for mind-blowing monstrosities in such films as *Scanners* (1980). Yet in both cases the choice was vindicated through the quality and success of the finished films.

A similar risk was taken with another

Brooksfilms production *My Favorite Year* (1982) which starred Peter O'Toole in splendid form as a swashbuckling actor buckling at the knees at the prospect of having to appear on live television. Interestingly the favorite year in question was 1954, the final year of Sid Caesar's *Your Show of Shows* and the young man who has to chaperone O'Toole's alcoholic hero is an ambitious young comedy writer (Mark Linn-Baker) with more than a passing resemblance to Mel Brooks himself. The risk was that the project was again entrusted to an unusual pair of hands, actor Richard Benjamin who was making his directing debut. He did not let the side down and his career behind the camera has continued to flourish.

Brooks should certainly be acknowledged for the encouraging and influential role he has played in the career of colleagues wanting to take the directing plunge themselves. Gene Wilder's *The Adventures of Sherlock Holmes' Smarter Brother* (1975), Marty Feldman's *The Last Remake of Beau Geste* (1977), Dom DeLuise's *Hot Stuff* (1979) and Anne Bancroft's *Fatso* (1980) are all comic dissertations that emanate from the Mel Brooks school of film-making and owe much

LEFT: A moment of desert action from Marty Feldman's *The Last Remake of Beau Geste*.

to his master's voice. The valuation placed on such a heritage and legacy, of course, is very much a matter of personal taste.

Some critics have blamed Brooks for initiating some of the baser trends in modern American comedy. When did wit and screwball ingenuity disappear from Hollywood comedy to be replaced by bad taste and nastiness? For the columnist Bart Mills it was either the moment when the shower curtain is pulled down while Hotlips is taking a shower in Robert Altman's *M*A*S*H* (1970) or the moment when Brooks anatomized the effect of beans in the campfire scene of *Blazing Saddles*. Yet it would be unfair to blame Brooks for the National Lampoons, or the Porkys, or the Police Academies, or horrendous excrescences like *Bachelor Party* (1984) or *Doin' Time* (1985). In Brooks's movies vulgarity is often very funny; in so many of his rivals's movies it is just vulgar.

Brooks must be used to being maligned by the critics by now, but it has not made him any the less sensitive to such attacks. Like a number of people within the industry he feels that film comedy has always been undervalued in terms of critical praise and prestigious awards. It saddens him particularly on behalf of his collaborators. By all accounts, he tells them at the outset that he will personally expect superb work from them, but they must resign themselves to the fact that, in all probability, it will not get the recognition it deserves. Admittedly he has guided performers like Gene Wilder and Madeline Kahn to Oscar nominations. Yet it is symptomatic that it was John Morris's serious score for *The Elephant Man* (with its heavy reliance on Barber's 'Adagio for Strings') that secured Morris an Oscar nomination, not his much more imaginative

ABOVE: Anne Bancroft and Dom DeLuise in *Fatso*, which was directed by Bancroft.

and audacious scores for Brooks's own comedies. Other collaborators whose work for Brooks has deserved more industry or award recognition would include writers like Ron Clark, Rudy DeLuca and Barry Levinson for their work on *Silent Movie*, and *High Anxiety*; an editor like Ralph Rosenblum for *The Producers*; a designer like Dale Hennessy for his superb sets for *Young Frankenstein*; and a choreographer like Alan Johnson for the memorable dance routines of *The Producers* and *History of the World – Part I.*

When defining the kind of teamwork necessary for the making of a motion picture, Brooks said mischievously, 'What you want in the end is a fraternal relationship in which you are the absolute boss.' For all the excellence of his team, ultimately Brooks is the *auteur* – as he defines it, the 'man with an idea, a concept, a philosophy who takes that idea from the vapor of inception to the final coalescence of it on film.' The films are basically a reflection of his outlook and it is interesting to see how that outlook has developed over the years. The themes – the need for fraternity, the futility of all forms of bigotry – have remained fairly constant. 'If I were to teach screenwriting,' he said once, 'I would teach one sentence: What do the leading characters *want*?' In the case of Brooks's films, the answer is simple: love.

There has undoubtedly been a change in the refinement of technique. There is a big advance from the rather haphazard camera set-ups in *The Producers* to the use of the camera in *High Anxiety* which provides one of the comic joys of the film. In terms of structure too, he has avoided some of the mistakes of *The Producers*, which give the film a rather lopsided shape, although whether he has solved all of his structural problems is still a moot point. It is not easy to pick out the best of Mel Brooks's films.

For me, the most consistently coherent and emotionally involving are *The Twelve Chairs* and *High Anxiety*, both comic and compassionate little parables of human weakness and yearning. Yet there are passages in his other films that are perhaps, more truly representative of Brooks at his most inimitable and brilliant – 'Springtime for Hitler' in *The Producers*, 'Puttin' on the Ritz' in *Young Frankenstein*, 'The Inquisition' in *History of the World – Part I*. These are classic set-pieces of modern movie comedy that will live in the memory.

Basically Brooks has never been a dramatist: he has always been first and foremost a clown. He has never sought the pathos or the philosophizing of a Chaplin or a Woody Allen; has never attempted to emulate the balletic grace of a Keaton or the dazzling dexterity with words of a Groucho Marx. He rarely makes you just smile; the response is either the groan or the guffaw. Yet his relentless gaiety comes from a passionate affirmation of life. The implicit message of some comedians is: Enjoy yourself – it's later than you think. Brooks's message is: Enjoy yourself – it's *better* than you think. And with the two new productions scheduled for release while this book is going to press, Alan Johnson's *Solar Warriors* and David Jones's *84 Charing Cross Road* (with Anne Bancroft and Anthony Hopkins), not to mention Brooks's

BELOW: Anne and Mel relax with the family.

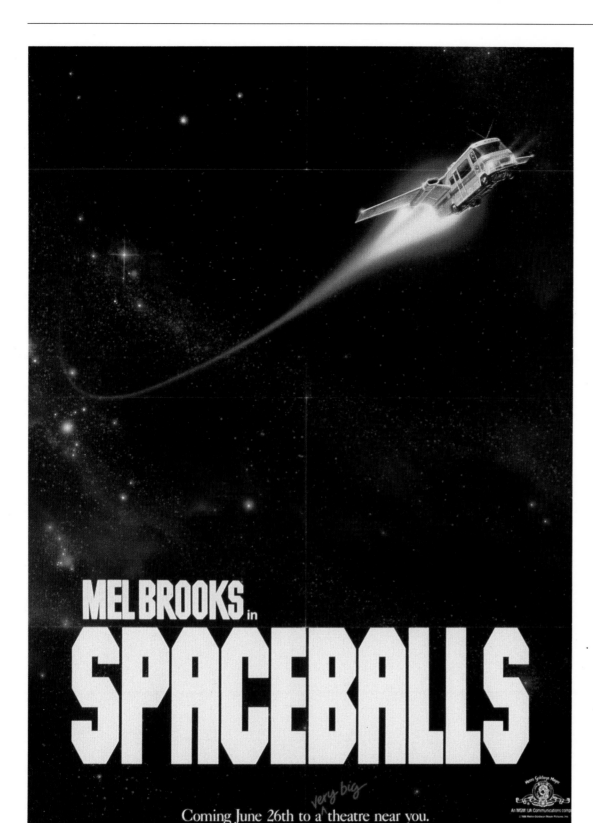

MEL BROOKS in
SPACEBALLS

Coming June 26th to a *very big* theatre near you.

own eagerly awaited sci-fi spoof *Spaceballs*, such optimism could well be justified.

When the grand old actor Edmund Gwenn was dying, he told a friend, 'It's not what I thought it would be like at all. It's hard. It's almost as hard as playing comedy.' We do tend to take our comedians too much for granted. It is a pleasure then to have this opportunity to thank Mel Brooks for the gift of laughter, and for many other things: for annihilating Nazism in *The*

Producers, routing racism in *Blazing Saddles*, and pillorying persecution in *History of the World – Part I*; for unearthing the 2000-Year-Old Man, for the first two hundred of which, he claimed, he was still being breast-fed; and for the discovery, not yet verified, that there were originally Fifteen Commandments, not Ten, and that William Shakespeare's middle name was 'Cohen.' May he long continue to deliver his 'dish of insanity.'

INDEX

Index

Page numbers in *italics* refer to illustrations

Acknowledgments

The publisher would like to thank Design 23 who designed this book, Wendy Sacks the editor, Mandy Little the picture researcher and Ron Watson who compiled the index. Our thanks also to the National Film Archive, London who supplied all the illustrations except for the following:

Alpha: pages 7, 9 (top).

Academy of Motion Picture Arts and Sciences: pages 18 (bottom), 19, 20 (top left), 21, 32, 65 (bottom), 67 (top), 71, 72 (bottom).

Aquarius, London: pages 8, 90.

Joel Finler Collection: pages 2 (bottom left), 12 (bottom), 13 (bottom), 17 (top), 33 (main picture), 35, 37 (bottom), 38-9, 57 (both), 58 (top), 59 (both), 61 (bottom), 63, 81 (bottom), 82 (right), 84 (both), 85 (bottom left), 90 (top).

Phototeque: pages 3 (bottom right), 4, 11, 12 (top), 13 (top), 14-15, 16, 20 (right), 34 (bottom), 47 (top), 51 (bottom), 54, 55, 56 (both), 83 (top), 85 (bottom right), 86 (bottom).

Syndication International: pages 1, 70 (bottom), 73 (both).

TPS/Keystone: page 94.